MOGGERHANGER PARK, BEDFORDSHIRE:

An Architectural and Social History from Earliest times to the Present

In memory of John Drake
who helped Moggerhanger,
fired the vision for the landscape
restoration and whose idea this book was
– and who died in 2012 while the
book was in preparation.

MOGGERHANGER PARK, BEDFORDSHIRE:

An Architectural and Social History from Earliest times to the Present

EDITED BY JANE BROWN & JEREMY MUSSON

CONTRIBUTIONS BY:

GARETH ATKINS

DAVID BAKER

JANE BROWN

PTOLEMY DEAN

JOHN DRAKE

PETER INSKIP

DAVID WATKIN

Published by Healeys Print Group on behalf of
Moggerhanger House Preservation Trust, 2012

Published by Healeys Print Group on behalf of
Moggerhanger House Preservation Trust, 2012

Text copyright © Moggerhanger House Preservation Trust, 2012
The moral right of the authors has been asserted.
Design and layout copyright © Healeys Print Group, 2012

Moggerhanger House Preservation Trust, The Park, Park Road,
Moggerhanger, Bedford, Bedfordshire, MK44 3RW
Email: mhpt@the-park.net
Website: www.mhpt.co.uk

Registered Charity Number:1064907

Printed and bound by Healeys Print Group, Ipswich

Paperback ISBN 978-0-9563162-5-7
Casebound ISBN 978-0-9563162-6-4

Front cover: The entrance of Moggerhanger House in 2012, Peter Packer.
Back cover: Humphrey Repton, Red Book (Moggerhanger), 1792, plate VI,
showing the first rebuild of Moggerhanger House by Soane, courtesy of
Lois Hunt Red Book Collection.

CONTENTS

The tribune revealed by Ptolemy Dean.

EDITOR'S FOREWORD

This collection of readable scholarly essays is published to celebrate the 2012 bi-centenary of the completion of Moggerhanger to designs by Sir John Soane. This house is a work of true originality but its artistic quality had been lost (to scholarship and to all wider appreciation) under layers of institutional use, and, after hospital use ended, subsequent decay.

Its recent restoration by architect Peter Inskip, supported by the Heritage Lottery Fund and English Heritage among others, has been rightly celebrated as a great achievement. This restoration project was initiated by the Christian charity Harvest Vision and passed on to the Moggerhanger House Preservation Trust. Works are ongoing to the accommodation and a new project to restore the Repton landscape has now begun.

The publication of this book is an important part of that story of revival. It is intended to record new scholarship and new understandings that have come to light in the process of the restoration of the house and in the serious preparation that has preceded the landscape restoration; moreover this book will help keep the cultural and aesthetic significance of this remarkable house to the fore.

The book covers all aspects of the story from the archaeology to the actual process of the restoration of the house itself, so often overlooked in such studies. In these pages all the layers of the story are laid out for us, of human imagination and endeavour, dreams and stark realities, joys and sorrows, which make up the story of a house, especially a dwelling place.

This book, the brainchild of John Drake, has been the work of many hands, and has also received vital support from The Paul Mellon Centre for Studies in British Art, Sir John Soane's Museum and the Marc Fitch Fund, the Alan Baxter Foundation, the Portrack Trust, the Nicholas and Judith Goodison Charitable Trust, Sir Richard MacCormac, RA, Sir Michael Hopkins, RA, and Lady (Patti) Hopkins, Helen Dorey and others – without whom it would not have been possible. The authors have been kind enough to waive any fees, so 100% of the sales of the book will go towards the maintenance and presentation of this important work of architecture.

Jeremy Musson

EDITOR'S NOTE

The Moggerhanger House Preservation Trustees originally asked me to write a social and design history of the house and park, to culminate in the restoration and redecoration: this I presented to them. However, it had become abundantly clear to me that the story of the house and its inhabitants had a parallel in the structural history – in the progress of Soane's creative thinking, the use and reuse of materials and the skills of the craftsmen who placed them – and that the restoration architect Peter Inskip was the best person to relate this second (or perhaps first) history.

Having such a rich and unusual picture of Moggerhanger's life, there was clearly an opportunity to add an opulent frame, an ambitious proposal to which the Trustees agreed. This framework is luxurious, by virtue of the distinction and generosity of the contributors. Every house needs its settlement and archaeological history, its place in the (famous) architect's career, the landscape history and, nowadays, some insight into the ethical pedigree of its owners. This is how this book came to take its present form.

Jane Brown

The entrance front, Ptolemy Dean.

LIST OF CONTRIBUTORS
(IN ALPHABETICAL ORDER)

GARETH ATKINS, BA, M.Phil., PhD, is British Academy Post-doctoral Fellow at Magdalene College, Cambridge. He works on religion and political culture in eighteenth- and nineteenth-century Britain, and is currently preparing a monograph on Anglican Evangelical networks in public life.

DAVID BAKER, OBE, MA, MIFA, FSA, IHBC, was Assistant History Master at Bedford School, then Conservation and Archaeology Officer in Bedfordshire County Planning Department 1972–1997, latterly involved in the difficult negotiations which led to the rescue of Moggerhanger house. He is currently a consultant on historic environment conservation.

JANE BROWN trained as a landscape architect, and since 1983, has been a writer and landscape historian whose books include *Gardens of a Golden Afternoon* (1982), *The Modern Garden* (2000) and *The Garden at Buckingham Palace* (2004). *The Omnipotent Magician*, her biography of Lancelot 'Capability' Brown, was published in 2011.

PTOLEMY DEAN, Dip. Arch, RIAS, RIBA, runs his own architectural practice Ptolemy Dean Architects, and was appointed Surveyor of Westminster Abbey in 2012; historic buildings expert for BBC 2's *Restoration*, he is also author of *Sir John Soane and the Country Estate* (1999), and *Sir John Soane and London* (2006).

JOHN DRAKE, MBE, MA Cantab, Dip. Arch. RIBA, Architectural Association Diploma in Conservation of Parks and Gardens, was Chairman of Cambridgeshire Gardens Trust, a Trustee of the Moggerhanger House Preservation Trust and a Royal Horticultural Society committee member and judge.

PETER INSKIP, MA Cantab, FSA, RIBA, is a partner in Peter Inskip + Peter Jenkins Architects, and was the project director for the restoration of Moggerhanger House. Other historic houses he has advised on include Chatsworth, Waddesdon and Stowe; his family has a long connection with east Bedfordshire.

JEREMY MUSSON, LLB (Hons), M.Phil., is an architectural historian and writer. Architectural Editor of *Country Life*, 1998–2007 and presenter of BBC2's *The Curious House Guest*, 2005–2007, his books, include *Up and Down Stairs* (2007) and *English Country House Interiors* (2011); he is also a trustee of the Moggerhanger House Preservation Trust.

DAVID WATKIN, MA Cantab, PhD LittD, Hon. FRIBA, FSA, is Emeritus Fellow of Peterhouse and Professor Emeritus at the University of Cambridge Department of the History of Art. His numerous publications include *Morality and Architecture Revisited* (2001), *The Architect King* (George III) (2004), *The Roman Forum* (2009); he has an especial interest in Sir John Soane and his period.

Views from before the restoration, above, below and following pages; The Eating Room.

The stables.

The corridors.

The kitchen.

Entrance hall.

Moggerhanger House: An Architectural Reflection

Ptolemy Dean

My first glimpse of Moggerhanger, in fading winter light, was from the back of Peter Inskip's car. I was one of his junior architectural assistants at the time, and as I recall, we swung past Moggerhanger on the way back from a site elsewhere. He had told me that he had worked on the house himself briefly when he was an assistant to Sir Albert Richardson, who had made modest alterations to what was then something akin to a Cottage hospital in the early 1960s.

Moggerhanger was a sorry sight. Conifer trees, long grass and unkempt asphalt drives led to Soane's front portico, attached to a house that had been 'snowcreted' in brilliant white, now smeared to a drab pigeon-effluent despoiled grey. Miserable wartime Nissen huts and municipal sodium street lights framed the scene and in what must once have been a park beyond, one or two battered old trees were hanging on against the inevitable deep ploughing of their roots. Planning consent had been given for the construction of houses in the park, and the house, an apparently awkward and listed incumbence on the site, was up for sale for a pound. The charity 'Harvest Vision' and the Moggerhanger House Preservation Trust have proved to be an excellent vehicle for achieving the repair and restoration of Moggerhanger, receiving significant grant aid and providing a sustainable and visionary use for the main house and its outbuildings.

Entering Moggerhanger in those days was never to be forgotten. The first sensation was hitting a wall of cold and damp. Condensation streamed down lime green painted walls and rusted surface mounted electrical conduits, to drip with melancholic irregularity onto linoleum floors curling up at the corners. But none of this, nor the faint smell of pee, could distract from an unfolding sequence of spaces that is amongst the finest I have yet to encounter in any building, whether it be by Soane or anyone else.

A low entrance hall led into an arcaded stair hall. Top lit from above, the eye was immediately taken up elegantly cantilevered stone stairs to a landing, beyond which could be glimpsed a semi-circular ante-chamber. But the temptation to ascend the stairs was immediately tempered by axial

The kitchen.

corridors at ground floor level with arched openings that appeared to extend telescopically to the left and also to the right. As any visitor to Sir John Soane's Museum in London will know, Soane's greatest skill is to offer an almost insatiable temptation to explore in all directions all at once.

Setting off down the corridor to the right, the first room on the left had been Soane's original dining room. Bereft of its fine columns, its ceiling was still set on differing planes to catch the available light in differing and subtle ways, with shadowing effects achieved by a variety of delicately moulded plaster cornices which not even the layers of thick hospital paint had destroyed. Natural light came through a pair of large south facing floor to ceiling sash windows with exquisitely fine glazing bars that looked out under an elegant veranda to the despoiled parkland beyond. This room was connected with the two drawing rooms, at that time knocked together to form a single ward. Despite this, one was immediately aware of how attractive in scale the house must have been to live in.

Returning to the passageway, a further sequence of arches, each becoming ever simpler, led, eventually, to the kitchen. This great volume of a room with a vast arched window, had been despoiled by abandoned fittings, suspended ceilings and "refenestration", but as a climax to this part of the route through the house, it revealed how even here, in the service areas, Soane was determined to maximise his architectural intent. What a contrast to the way service areas are so often treated today.

The staircase hall.

The Landing.

The Boudoir.

With dusk consuming the unlit building there was time only for one last architectural sally, quickly up the stairs to discover what lay beyond that semi-circular ante room that had been glimpsed from the entrance hall. Out of the shadows could be found an enchanting former boudoir with a gently curved cornice, rounded corners and very deep window reveals to a segmental headed window. Soane's detail mouldings to the shutters contrasting with the much plainer but nevertheless discrete 1960s fittings added in a more austere era.

Moggerhanger has now been transformed and revealed; new subtleties exposed and uncovered, but that moment of its first discovery remains with me eternally.

MOGGERHANGER PARK:
THE RISE AND FALL AND REBIRTH
OF A COUNTRY HOUSE

JANE BROWN

ONE

*W*atchful strangers travelling along the Great North Road or on the railway between Biggleswade and Sandy are easily deluded into a Noel Cowardism, 'Very flat, Bedfordshire',* but they could not be more mistaken. Approaching Sandy both the road, in its modern guise as the A1(T), and the London to Edinburgh railway line hug the course of the river Ivel in preparation for the Sandy gap through the steep greensand ridge. The traveller with the leisure to look eastwards from Sandy will see – as Humphry Repton saw just over 200 years ago – 'the little corner of Hasells-hall embosomed in its venerable woods' where the ridge rises steeply.[1] In the opposite direction the westward view is across fields reminiscent of their productive past but now mostly bereft of an abundance of vegetables and salads for local and London dinner tables. In the middle distance the dark bulk of ancient Sheerhatch Wood rises to mark the resumption of the ridge, and immediately adjacent to Sheerhatch, on the bowsprit of the scarp, is Moggerhanger Park.

Reciprocal views across the landscape were the delight of eighteenth-century designers, the perfect expression of the fashionable desire to live on the free-draining sandy uplands and enjoy the *prospect* of the valley. Today, walkers on the Greensand Ridge Path can experience Repton's designer's eye view as they descend from near Sheerhatch down to Northill, cross the road, river and railway at Sandy and climb to the eastern scarp by Hasells Hedge.** On the reverse, east to

* Originally: 'Very flat, Norfolk' from Coward's *Private Lives*, 1933.
** In *Sentimental Journey* (1998), tracing an outline of family history, Francis Pym rationalised the many spellings of his home to The Hazells, but the OS map still has Hasells Hedge and Repton's spelling has also been kept in quotations from his Red Books.

west journey down from the Everton scarp and across the valley to Sheerhatch, the situation of Moggerhanger Park – the *raison d'être* for the architect John Soane's design of the house – can be appreciated almost in the manner of two centuries' ago (fig. 1).

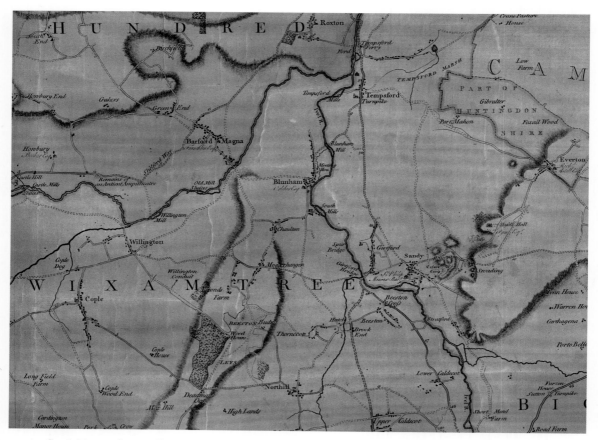

fig. 1 Extract from Jeffery's *Bedfordshire*, 1765, showing the River Ivel cutting through the greensand scarps; on the right, east of Sandy, is the Everton ridge, in the centre is Blunham, and to the south of this Moggerhanger and Sheerhatch wood sit on the western ridge.

This story of Moggerhanger Park colours the social history of eastern Bedfordshire and also the larger world. The house as we see it was built in the period from 1790 to 1815, 'carefully reconsidered and adjusted over the years into a great work of architecture'[2] for Godfrey Thornton and his son Stephen. The Thorntons were City merchants with an extensive family connection to the Bank of England, of which Godfrey was governor during the 1790s, and thus it was no accident that his architect was also the Bank's architect. For Soane, the rebuilding of the fortress in

Threadneedle Street – that 'pile of national greatness' – was the 'pride and boast' of his life and the core of his self-belief as an architect.[3] Consequently, he did his very best for the Thorntons, and in the context of the times a country house by Soane, set amidst drives, plantations and gardens planned by Humphry Repton, the leading landscape improver of the day, was the *dernier cri*, the last word in elegance and fashion.

How and why the Thorntons and their celebrity designers came to this quiet corner of rural Bedfordshire will be revealed in the following pages. The priority here is to deal with the question of that unique and curious name: Moggerhanger, or Muggerhanger as it was when Godfrey Thornton acquired it, which rather prompts us to think of a scruffy black cat or an unpleasant street crime. It is, though, a very ancient name, recorded as 'Mogarhangre' in the early thirteenth century, later Moggehangre – the second half from the Old English *hangra* (hanger) for a sloping wood, a wood on the side of a hill. The hill in question is the ridge of the Lower Greensand, completely wooded in the Domesday survey, making the present Sheerhatch wood a relict of tree cover that extended along the whole of the spur and included the site of the present park.

The spelling continued to vary, with the 'k' creeping in, as in Mokerhanger, from *muker*, a miser, or *mukeren*, to hoard, which invites romantic imaginings. Did some medieval man of the woods find treasure left by the Romans who passed this way, or was there a legendary hoard from attacks on rich pilgrim travellers to Warden Abbey? In the seventeenth century early maps were marked Morehanger, then by the mid-eighteenth century it seemed to settle as Muggerhanger, as Mr Skinner and Co., of Aldersgate Street, London called it in the 1784 sale particulars. John Soane seemed to vary Moggerhanger and Muggerhanger and Humphry Repton, whose fleeting passage from place to place often left him with mistaken impressions, used Mogenhanger in the introduction to his Red Book of 28 May 1792. On Bryant's 1825–6 *Map of Bedfordshire* it is definitely Moggerhanger, as it is in the 1857 sale particulars, and which the Ordnance Survey adopted, despite the later nineteenth-century owners, the Dawkins', preference for Morhanger. For a while this genteel Morhanger embraced the park and the village, and the new church, St John the Evangelist, which Mrs Dawkins had built in 1860–1. Then in 1919 the plans for the County Sanatorium used Mogerhanger House, though in practice it became Park Hospital, and everyone else reverted to Moggerhanger, as it has remained. However, it is noticeable that people born and bred in the area still pronounce it *Muggerhanger*.[4]

EARLY HISTORY: 'A CAPITAL AND VERY VALUABLE ESTATE'
Moggerhanger is part of a close-knit countryside strongly reliant on the underlying geology. The park occupies a unique position, above the fifty-metre contour line of the spur of the greensand ridge, where it is broken by the river Ivel on its way to join the Great Ouse at Tempsford. The surrounding countryside is made up of the seven parishes of the ancient Hundred of Wixamtree, or 'Wihstan's tree', which marked the meeting place of the elders, and is thought to be Deadman's Oak, still indicated at the ancient crossing of routes at the south-east corner of Sheerhatch Wood.[5] In traditional manner the parishes of Cardington, Cople and Willington were marked out

across the grain of the land from the Ouse-side pastures to the greensand ridge; Blunham parish, bounded by the Ouse and the Ivel, extends southwards and upwards to the Moggerhanger spur, and the east–west parishes of Northill, Old Warden and Southill are on the undulating land between the ridge and the Ivel. The pattern of minor roads that we still use emphasises this age-old organisation.

Medieval Moggerhanger was part of the manor of Chalton, in the parish of Blunham, where the church's spacious south porch was traditionally built and maintained by Moggerhanger people for their own use: baptisms and funerals could be conducted in the porch, which also gave shelter after their cross-country journey to worship.[6] The community was almost exclusively tenant farmers and labourers, but cultivation was sparse and sporadic. The land itself figures as the currency of marriage settlements and exchanges among manorial lords. History came close but never quite touched the sandy slopes: in

fig. 2 Blunham, St Edmund and St James, memorial to Thomas and Margaretta Bromsall.

1541 King Henry VIII stayed with his good friend Sir John Gostwick at Willington, having awarded the Gostwicks the lands of Warden Abbey; late Elizabethan enclosures sparked fights in Blunham and Tempsford; the rector of Everton, Andrew Byng, was one of the scholars who worked on the text of King James I's Authorised Version of the Bible, and the poet John Donne was famously rector of Blunham, though largely an absentee. Did Moggerhanger men go with Sir Samuel Luke from Cople to garrison Newport Pagnell for the Parliamentarians in 1640s? Did they, like many Bedfordshire men, creep home again in dismay at the killing of the king? Thomas Tompion, the son of the Ickwell blacksmith, found fame and fortune at the court of Charles II for his clocks and timepieces, which were to marshal Time itself in the Royal Observatory at Greenwich.

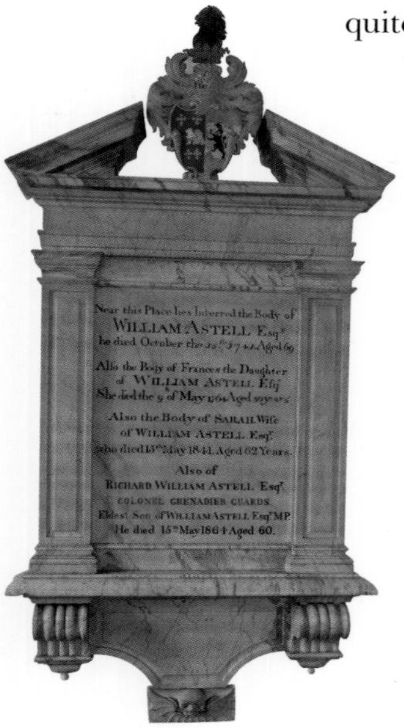

Then, out of the mists of uncertainty, comes a name firmly linked to Moggerhanger, that of Thomas Bromsall, Armiger, lord of Blunham and Moggerhanger. Thomas died in 1682 and lies in Blunham church, with his wife, Margaretta Orlebar of Hinwick (*c*.1624–64) (fig. 2). Thomas and Margaretta Bromsall had three children that we

fig. 3 Everton, St Mary's, memorial to William Astell, d.1741.

know of: a daughter Margaretta who is buried with the Orlebars at Hinwick, and two sons, Ralph or Randolph (1649–93) and Thomas (1651–1705). Of greater importance here is their grandson, Owen Thomas Bromsall, who married Elizabeth Astell (1703–47), the only child of William Astell (1672–1741) of Everton (fig. 3). Owen Thomas was to be the last of his name – a name perpetuated in Bromsall's Piece marked on old maps of Everton – and when he died in 1731 he was given a funeral of some pomp, with pall-bearers, at Northill.[7] All the considerable Bromsall properties passed to his father-in-law William Astell, presumably in accordance with Elizabeth Astell's marriage settlement, and designed to protect the Astell interest in the Bromsall lands, should Elizabeth marry for a second time. She did, to Humphrey Monoux of Sandy Place, but for much of her last ten years she lived at Wootton, the Monoux estate south-west of Bedford, where she died (fig. 4).

fig. 4 Wootton, St Mary's which has Monoux family memorials.

So, there is Moggerhanger, firmly within the property portfolio of the acquisitive William Astell, who had bought the Everton estate from the last of the Careys in 1713. His home was at Everton House, which then stood on the south side of St Mary's churchyard. His holdings ranged from Hail Weston north of St Neots to Tempsford and Biggleswade, and now Blunham, Beeston and Northill. William Astell made a second marriage, to Mary Bagnall, and they had a son and a daughter. This son, Richard Astell (1717–77) (fig. 5) inherited everything at his father's death in 1741, including Moggerhanger. He enjoyed his lands and did his duties as a county gentleman, a colonel of the Huntingdon Militia, Justice of the Peace and a deputy-lieutenant of Bedfordshire. In the autumn of 1756, childless and approaching his fortieth year, he stood as godfather to Francis, the fifth child of his neighbours William and Elizabeth Pym at The Hazells.

fig. 5 Richard Astell, 1717–1777 (artist unknown).

Richard's father William Astell had tried to buy The Hazells in 1720 for himself but without success; this neighbouring estate at Everton was bought by Heylock Kingsley, whose daughter Elizabeth had married William Pym. This first neighbourly connection between the Astells and the Pyms will echo down the years in the Moggerhanger story. [8]

Richard Astell, according to the memorial his widow placed in St Mary's church at Everton, was a man of 'numerous virtues… general benevolence and blameless manners', but he had no heir from his two marriages (fig. 7). At his death in 1777, as their wily and far-seeing father's will decreed, everything was to go to his sister Margaret or her heirs. Margaret Astell had died in her late thirties in 1753, not long after the death of her husband Godfrey Thornton of Clapham (1701–51): *this* Godfrey, was a younger brother of the Robert Thornton (1692–1748) who had moved south from Hull to establish the family's fortunes as a Russia merchant in the City of London while living at the then rural village of Clapham. Godfrey, like Robert, was a director of the Bank of England, and because of his City involvements he and Margaret lived mostly away from Bedfordshire, in Clapham and apparently at a house in Kensington, where they had reared five sons, three of whom lived to become part of the Moggerhanger story (figs. 8a and b).

Their eldest, William (1734–1801), married to his cousin, Elizabeth Thornton, was his uncle's heir, provided that he assumed the additional surname and arms of Astell (fig. 6). He duly became William

figs. 6 and 7 Everton, St Mary's, memorials to William Thornton Astell and his wife Elizabeth (left) and to Richard Astell (right).

Thornton Astell and settled to life as a country squire while maintaining his City merchant interests. William and Elizabeth lived at Everton House, until they were laid to rest in the church, William aged sixty-seven in 1801 and Elizabeth aged seventy-three in 1809. They had no children.

Godfrey and Margaret's second son, Robert Thornton (1735–1803), inherited well over a thousand acres at Moggerhanger as a sporting estate and seems to have had the use of it during his uncle's lifetime. Jeffrey's *Map of Bedfordshire* (1765) shows a house called Almond's Farm (possibly a corruption of Almoner's a monastic relic, as in Palmer's Wood south of Deadman's Oak?) on the site

fig. 8 (a) Godfrey Thornton of Clapham d.1751, by Isaac Wood, 1735 and, (b) (right) Margaret Astell, the heiress who brought Moggerhanger to the Thorntons.

of the present house, but this name was soon lost as Robert Thornton changed the farm into the 'convenient and modernized' Muggerhanger Lodge.[9] The Lodge was a brick house, limewashed, of two storeys with sash windows underneath dormers in a tiled roof. It was a typical sporting man's retreat, the main room being the twenty-five by nineteen feet dining room, for evening-long dinners of boiled beef and pheasant pies washed down with port, beside a roaring log fire. On the opposite side of the 'genteel Entrance Hall' were two smaller rooms, one a little parlour, the province of the ladies should they wish to be present. There were seven bedrooms and 'good offices', the resident servants' quarters so essential to the sporting life. The gamekeeper, William Tatman, whose family were farmers in Blunham, was living at the Lodge when it was put up for sale in 1784, and so it seems likely that Mrs Tatman acted as cook/housekeeper.

The main approach drive to the Lodge came from the south, from the Budna and Northill road, and the stable block was on the east side of the house, with additional lodgings for grooms. The immediate surroundings of some sixty-six acres did not aspire to be called a park, but there was 'a shrubbery' – a new term not yet in common use – a kitchen garden with a 'lofty' fruit wall, an orchard, and Garden Wood was laid out 'with rural and pleasing walks'.[10]

Robert Thornton did not enjoy his sporting lodge for long and some explanation may be found in his family life. He had married his cousin, Sarah Thornton, from Hull, who died shortly after the birth of their son, Richard, in 1764. Richard died when he was ten, dashing his father's hopes of shared country pursuits at Muggerhanger Lodge. Clearly deeply affected, Robert Thornton did not remarry until 1778, and his new wife was Elizabeth Warner of Hatton Garden in the heart of London. It seems perfectly possible that Elizabeth disliked Muggerhanger Lodge and refused to bury herself in the Bedfordshire countryside, and Robert was content to leave his disappointments behind.

For whatever reason, Robert Thornton put the estate up for sale by auctioneer Mr Skinner, at the famous Garraway's Coffee House, the meeting house of merchants in 'Change Alley in the City', the sale to take place on 6 May 1784[11] (fig. 9). The whole Moggerhanger estate was revealed as a tempting prospect: 1,400 acres, six miles in diameter, five farms and the invaluable fishing rights to a three-mile stretch of the Ouse and Ivel. The detailed prospectus was printed but whether the auction actually took place is not known, nor is there any apparent record of a sale or even a private treaty. What is certain is that Godfrey Thornton (1737–1805), the younger brother of William and Robert, became the owner of Moggerhanger, but because of family negotiations and the pressures of City business he paid little attention to it for more than six years.

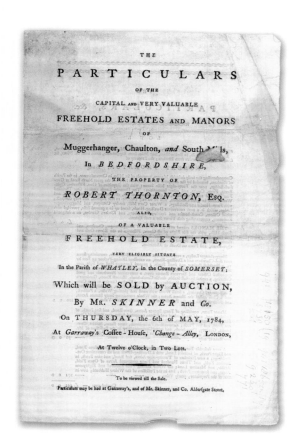

fig. 9 Particulars for the proposed sale at Garraway's Coffee-House, 6th May 1784; Lot 1 described Muggerhanger Lodge as a 'very convenient modernised Residence' with seven bedrooms, a dressing-room, a large dining-parlour, small study and a breakfast-room, a butler's pantry, kitchen and offices, and outside a kitchen garden, fruit room, orchard, shrubbery and a small wood with 'rural and pleasing walks', the whole just over 60 acres and a yearly value of £100.

THE OWNERS OF MOGGERHANGER PARK

With the dates of their ownership:

THOMAS BROMSALL of Blunham, d.1682, owned the Estate and Manorial rights. They passed to his grandson

|

OWEN THOMAS BROMSALL d.1731 m Elizabeth, daughter of William Astell (below)

❖

WILLIAM ASTELL 1731–1741 by marriage settlement of his daughter Elizabeth by his first wife;
He married secondly Mary Bagnall. Their son

|

RICHARD ASTELL of Everton House 1741–1777 d.s.p
married firstly his cousin Sarah Bagnall and married secondly Hannah Kennet who subsequently married
Mr Pownall. Richard's sister Margaret Astell d.1753 m Godfrey Thornton of Clapham who d.1751, and had
three sons, William Thornton Astell of Everton, Robert Thornton and Godfrey Thornton.
By the will of Hannah Pownall (above) it went to their second son

|

ROBERT THORNTON of Muggerhanger Lodge, thence to his younger brother Godfrey in 1784

|

GODFREY THORNTON of Moggerhanger House d.1805 m Jane Godin, their eldest son

|

STEPHEN THORNTON of Moggerhanger House 1805–1850 m Mary Littledale, their son

|

Colonel GODFREY THORNTON of Moggerhanger House d.1857 sold by his executors to

|

Rev EDWARD HENRY DAWKINS d.1859 m ELIZABETH d.1863, their son

|

EDWARD HENRY FREDERICK DAWKINS of Morhanger Park m Louisa Barnett,
by transfer 1885 to

|

RICHARD MERCER, d.1904, to his son

|

Colonel ALGERNON MERCER by private sale 1907 to

|

SYDNEY and SELINA VIOLET FANE, requisitioned 1914

|

GODWIN COLLEGE, Cliftonville, Margate, evacuation 1915–1919

|

BEDFORDSHIRE COUNTY COUNCIL purchased in 1919 and set up the County Sanatorium 1919–1948

|

Bedfordshire County Council/BEDFORD GROUP HOSPITAL MANAGEMENT COMMITTEE, [NHS} Park
Hospital, 1948–1987 sold by tender to

|

[TWIGDEN HOMES Ltd] sold to

|

HARVEST VISION for £1 in 1994, thence gifted to

|

MOGGERHANGER HOUSE PRESERVATION TRUST founded 1997

fig. 10 (a) Godfrey Thornton, d.1805 by Sir William Beechey, and **(b)** his wife Jane Godin.

GODFREY THORNTON AND JOHN SOANE, 1790–1805

The new owner of Moggerhanger, Godfrey Thornton, had enjoyed a privileged life; brought up amidst his prosperous Thornton and Astell connections, he had served as a colonel in the Grenadier Guards before selling out at about the time of his thirtieth birthday, and marrying Jane Godin of Cullands Grove in Middlesex (fig. 10b). Jane was the daughter of a City merchant and a suitable partner for Godfrey, who now assumed his rightful place in the Thornton City interests, with his office in Austin Friars. There the main business was the underwriting of shipping insurance and the financing of trading and development loans especially in the Russian and Baltic trades, in alliance with the family's enterprises with the Wilberforces in Hull. He had become a director of the Bank of England in 1772, when he was thirty-five; at that time directors served for two-year terms with a compulsory year's break in between, and he was to serve seven terms until 1801, becoming deputy-governor in 1791–3, and governor 1793–5. He was thus in his fifties, a City man busily burdened with private and public concerns, when he acquired his country estate; he was certainly no countryman. Godfrey's portrait by Sir William Beechey suggests a good-natured if shrewd businessman (and displays an almost brotherly likeness to Beechey's contemporary portrait of George III) but perhaps the taciturn financier was uppermost for Godfrey Thornton has apparently left no cache of letters or papers that allow posterity to round out his personality[12] (fig. 10a).

Godfrey's father had built the Thornton refinery in Hull and so it becomes evident that they were part of the transatlantic sugar trade, (i.e. the slave trade) and in Godfrey's case shipping sugar cane on to St Petersburg, where, though Catherine the Great wished to improve the conditions of the serfs, labour was slavery by any other name. It appears that Godfrey Thornton was an enlightened merchant, he was a member of the Sierra Leone Company which established the settlement for freed

fig. 11 John Soane 1753–1837, by William Owen, 1804.

slaves,[13] and – as the Thorntons were essentially clannish – he cannot have been unaware of his Clapham (Sect) cousins' evangelicalism and their efforts to improve working conditions for all men and women. Godfrey Thornton was clearly a formidable man: in 1789 he became a member of the Bank of England's building committee, and so came face to face with the Bank's architect, appointed the previous year, John Soane. Soane was thirty-five, described by his biographer Gillian Darley as 'tall and bonily thin, with an intense, uncertain gaze'[14] (fig. 11). Only eight years into his solo architectural practice, he was setting out on the greatest challenge of his career, the Bank's rebuilding scheme. Peter Inskip, the architect of Moggerhanger's present restoration, imagines that the temperamental, highly strung Soane must have found it irritating to have to travel to Bedfordshire and 'the obscure little lodge' at Godfrey Thornton's request, but how could he refuse? Soane eventually managed two days in mid-November 1790, opening his journal account to Godfrey Thornton with charges of £2. 12s. 0d. for his visit and making plans and measured survey sketches. The joy of Soane's work is that so many of his journals, accounts and drawings have survived in his legacy to us, his home and museum at 13 Lincoln's Inn Fields in London, and this single circumstance has made the restoration of Moggerhanger Park possible.[15]

From the outset – though it was a slow start – Soane's journal entries reveal his characteristic 'ushering' of his client, from a modest beginning to a much more ambitious building. The architect made a second visit in September 1791 and during the following winter he prepared his plans and working drawings. He proposed turning the lodge around by 90 degrees – making the entrance on the east front, leaving the south front free for the garden façade, and adding another wing to achieve the symmetrical gabled entrance front that Humphry Repton illustrated (plate VI) in his Red Book of 1792 (figs. 12 and 13). The priority was practical, the old stables east of the house were demolished and Soane's new stables built on the west side. The plans for these new stables were 'settled' with Godfrey Thornton in early 1792 – a two-storeyed block flanked by carriage houses in single-storey wings – and most of the construction work to the house and new stables was accomplished that year. Soane was paid £500 on account in November 1792 and another £500 in August 1793.*

Soane's fertile flow of ideas for the interiors of the now L-shaped house continued. The bluff Godfrey Thornton would have scorned aesthetic notions – he *paid* his architect for those – but he did love his wife Jane, they had been married for almost thirty years, and this love was expressed in the most charming of architectural conceits, the delicately detailed and decorated room over the

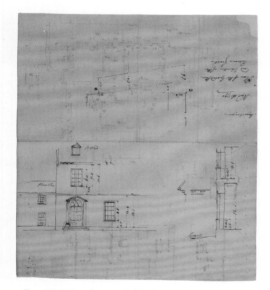

fig. 12 John Soane, initial survey dated 16th November 1790 of 'Muggerhanger' lodge, three storeys, built of brick, limewashed, with a stylish pedimented front door and gothic fanlight.

fig. 13 Humphry Repton, Red Book 1792, plate VI, showing Soane's first house with the entrance on the east front.

* A reference to 'Mr Holland' being given working drawings for the portico in April 1793 suggests that the builders were the Hollands' family firm, which was under the control of the architect Henry Holland, in whose office Soane had served his pupillage.[16]

new entrance porch, known as Mrs Thornton's dressing room.** From the first this was the gem of Moggerhanger's rooms, elegantly proportioned, painted in soft grey with a blue clouded ceiling, and details of the mouldings picked out and gilded. The dressing room was next to Soane's new best bedroom for the Thorntons, with other bedrooms along the south garden front.

Downstairs the old sportsmen's dining room became the new Eating Room, on the south-east corner of the house. This Eating Room and the new drawing room across the hall – called by Peter Inskip 'a remarkable drawing room with a splayed arch-headed window' – were both light and airy and distempered in soft colours: pale violet or mauve in the drawing room, with beige in the Eating Room. All the work, especially the plasterwork and decoration, was of the highest 'London' quality, Soane sending his best decorators to do the work.[17]

Godfrey Thornton settled Soane's final account for this first stage of alterations – a total of £2,021. 5s. 4d. including the sums on account – on 22 April 1795, and that year the Thorntons spent the first of their summer sojourns at Moggerhanger. Though it was a charming retreat it was a small house for such a rich man, and within two years both architect and clients were chafing for improvements. In the summer of 1797, in June, Soane booked himself on to the famous coach *Highflier* to Biggleswade, and stayed the night at Moggerhanger, talking over his plans for more alterations. The next day Godfrey Thornton accompanied him to Southill, where the remodelling by Soane's former master, Henry Holland, for Samuel Whitbread II was nearing completion; Soane continued on his way by chaise to Tyringham Park, where he was also working. Godfrey Thornton, having found a great interest in agricultural advances and in building model cottages on his estate, presumably discussed these things with his progressive neighbour, Mr Whitbread.[18]

————————

ENTER MR REPTON

[Mr Rushworth of Sotherton:] 'It wants improvement, ma'am . . . I hope I shall have some good friend to help me.'
'Your best friend upon such an occasion,' said Miss Bertram calmly, 'would be Mr Repton, I imagine'.
That is what I was thinking . . . I had better have him at once. His terms are five guineas a day.[19]

It was the nature of architecture that John Soane's visits to Moggerhanger were rare and fleeting; others lingered longer, and we have an eye-witness to the creation of the house and park in the Honourable John Byng (1743–1813) who was brought up at Southill and liked to return each summer

** Not called the boudoir until after Jane Thornton's time.

for an extended ramble in his native countryside. His favourite hostelry – unavailingly good, of the cheapest and quietest – was the Sun at Biggleswade, the 'old shop' as he called it, where he would install his family party for weeks on end.[20] Byng humanises our countryside; he relished banquets of eel and roasted rabbit, apricot tarts and custards, he primed the locals on the best fishing holes and safest bathing pools, and with his young son, Frederick, he loved to spend days by the languid summer rivers. He was a sharp observer – of 'the culture brought to great perfection' of fields of carrots, cucumbers, peas, parsnips and beans beside the turnpike road between Sandy and Girtford Bridge; of the 'newly repaired house of Mr T[hornton) upon the hill at Muggerhanger'. Byng despaired that 'the best taste and first fortune' could never bring it to beauty and comfort; it wanted water, soil and timber.[21]

Byng also noted the earliest enclosures and on more than one occasion 'broke down some rails courageously' – nostalgia made him conservative, and his sympathies were with the country people oppressed by the run of miserable summers and left with fields of flattened, sprouting, unharvested corn, one poor man 'dying under fatigue, reaping away in a field of twenty acres'.[22]

In late May 1792 the redoubtable Byng arrived at the Sun; he woke to a fine Monday morning and he intended to ride 'but Mr Repton – the now noted landscape gardener – came in' and delayed him for half an hour! He took vengeance in his diary that night: 'he is a gentleman I have long

fig. 14 Humphry Repton's Trade Card, engraved by T. Medland, explaining his profession.

known, and of so many words that he is not easily shaken off; he asserts so much, and assumes so much, as to make me irritable, for he is one (of the many) who is never wrong; and therefore why debate with him?' Repton had returned to the inn at 9 o'clock having been out all day surveying, and yet – for Byng did not miss much – at 8 o'clock next morning, 29 May, he was up and off again 'to Mr T's in this neighbourhood, where he is to plan and oversee'.[23]

Humphry Repton was a genial fellow with a good eye for a gentleman and never missed an opportunity to forward his profession. He was just forty, a year older than John Soane[24] and yet their lives and their personalities could not have been more different. Though equally energetic and hard-working, Repton was rather emotional, and inclined to whimsicality – an asset to the role of landscape gardener, a professional name he had concocted for himself – believing that the many reversals in his life showed the hand of Providence steering him towards his eventual success. In fact, Soane and Repton are the perfect alter egos of their professional psyches, the one conjuring interior lights and comforts from hard materials, the other equally susceptible to the shadows and the sunlight across well-manicured but bosky acreages.

Repton was also different in that he had nothing to do with London; he was essentially a countryman. His base was a modest rented house at Hare Street in Essex, where he settled his wife, Mary, and their family, and from where he advertised his profession. His elegant trade card, drawn by himself (engraved by T. Medland), with its image of the masterful surveyor in his brimmed beaver hat, was instantly recognisable. It was an early example of a successful 'logo' and he inserted it into all his Red Books (fig. 14). A Red Book, his *coup de grâce*, was prepared for each client, a slim volume bound in red morocco (though later many were brown calf) which appealed equally to the landowner in his estate office and the ladies in the drawing room. Each had an explanatory copperplate text with watercolour illustrations enlivened by Repton's unique 'slides'. Additional pieces of cartridge paper attached by a tongue of card were glued on the reverse of the page and placed over the watercolour; the existing view was painted on the slide, which when folded back would reveal the new, improved vista achievable under his directions.

Repton opened his Red Book for 'Mogenhanger' as he called it by assuring Godfrey Thornton – as he did so many others – 'that altho' Landscape Gardening is often considered as more subject to fashion or caprice than any other Art, it is not less reducible to rules than Architecture or Painting since the true Taste in all the Arts must be founded on reason and reflection'.[25] He noted that his first visit was on 28 May 1792 – he does not say whether there were additional visits – but his plan or scheme was completed in August.[26]

His first impression of Moggerhanger was disappointing, but then he often liked to sound professionally pert and disappointed. It was perhaps unfortunate that his opinion of the area had been formed the previous year, working for Francis Pym at The Hazells, which fitted Repton's ideal of a Palladian 'constant residence set in a park of interesting undulations' (fig. 15). Repton had a definite hierarchy, at the top the ducal estate, then the constant residence, followed by the sporting seat and the villa. Soane's white-gabled Moggerhanger hardly conformed to the 'superior stile'; he found it 'too large and too much ornamented' for a farmhouse, but too humble for a family's country-seat, and it was too far from London town to be called a villa. He settled on 'an occasional sporting seat', promising to avoid any suggested improvements that would interfere with future additions 'to give it more importance of Character'.[27]

While allowing for the difficulties, Repton wrote, 'where Genius is confined to the altering of an old house' Soane's new drawing room gave Repton a problem, in that it was too close to the Entrance, and its low window exposed its view 'to the occasional defilement of Horses waiting at the door'.[28] Much time and debate were to be given to this problem of the horses, and Repton's solution was that the drive should dwindle to 'a neat gravel walk' under the drawing room windows, and be looped away from the house behind a shrub bed so that the coach could wait at a discreet distance. Repton loved looping drives, they are one of his trademarks; as his plan shows the loop allowed the coach or chaise to return to the new stables, or leave via his new drive which passed between two giant elms, 'the finest features in the whole place', and on out to the Bedford road[29] (figs. 16 and 17).

Inside the house he was also concerned about the views from the Eating Room, which he imagined would be used also for breakfasts and as a family sitting room. In the novels of Jane Austen, and the equally authentic Georgette Heyer, the drawing room was only ever for visitors, and mother and daughters are always found sitting in the breakfast parlour. Soane's Eating Room had the lovely view to the south-east across the fields of Beeston Leasows. Repton lowered the park pale, effectively

fig. 15 Repton's Red Book 'at Hasells Hall' 1791, the view westwards to Moggerhanger.
Fig. 18 shows Repton's reciprocal view from Moggerhanger.

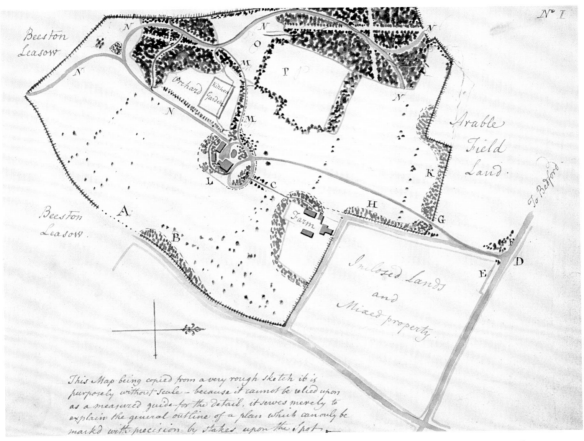

fig. 16 Repton's Red Book 'Mogenhanger' 1792, Plan of Proposals, 'copied from a very rough sketch it is purposely without scale', with details noted as follows:

A = the break in the park pale to allow the views to the Royston hills;
B = screen planting to hide cornfield, Mr Thornton should buy this land to control the view;
C = footpath to the Farm which is screened but still a desirable neighbour;
D = here the drive meets the Bedford road; with thickly planted areas at E and F;
G = the site for the gothic entrance lodge;
H = screening for farm buildings seen from the entrance drive; (no I and J);
K = planting to 'close' park views to/from arable land;
L = is the line of a ha-ha to allow meadow to be grazed;
M = leisure walks, with N = drives to Garden Wood and views out of the park, especially at
the corner of Beeston Leasow with the view to Northill church;
O and P = are paddocks, the harsh boundaries to be broken up.

N. B. Repton's principles of screening and viewpoints are implicit in the landscape restoration scheme.

fig. 17 Repton's Red Book 'Mogenhanger' 1792, showing (top) the rather desolate entrance from the Bedford road, and (bottom) the flap folded back showing the double-staged entrance to the new lodge which is more inviting.

making a ha-ha, so that the house lawn could melt into the view, but he was worried that the fields were owned by a neighbour, Samuel Sutton of St John's, and might easily be planted with corn. Repton thought corn 'incompatible' with lawns, whether it was the seasonal change or the too-close proximity of labourers that offended his sensibilities is not clear, but he recommended Godfrey Thornton to acquire and thus control the Leasows, which Thornton did.[30] Repton also thought that the impression of a happy village was the best recommendation as to the character of his client and though Moggerhanger village performed well in this respect, with cottages 'already in very neat repair', it only wanted a few honeysuckles and vines to decorate their walls and some evergreens to unite raggedly detached buildings for all to be perfect.[31] Finally, in his well-meant but interfering manner, he allowed that driving out was a pleasure for the elderly and invalid, the motivation for his gravelled walks that doubled as drives and led to viewpoints. In addition, he proposed the entrance drive should be continued across the Bedford road from his new entrance and over Willow Hill to the river, where, he thought, there could be a fishing cottage for the use of guests.

At the house, now given presence by its framework of drives and shrubberies, he fenced in a garden on the east and south sides – 'for flowers and neat dressed ground' – and indicated a gravel walk passing the greenhouse[32] to visit the kitchen garden, or to skirt the walls to Garden Wood. Repton was no plantsman but he had strong views about appropriate planting: his plantings had a definite hierarchy, allowing flowering shrubs, lilacs and philadelphus were great favourites, near the house but only more robust forestry species, hollies, yew, box, laurels and evergreen oaks, in the woodland. Spruce, laburnums, privets and thorns could be used to screen service buildings. In the woodland, the gravelled walks or drives led to views, his 'bursts' out of the trees carefully aligned to the best views – north-westwards across the valley to Cardington, southwards to Northill church and eastwards to The Hazells on the opposite ridge. Repton, knowing of the Thorntons' long connections and old friends at Everton, seemed to want to perpetuate the link across the Ivel valley: 'the little corner of Hasells-hall embosomed in its venerable woods, is doubtless the finest distant object that can be obtained in Mogenhanger park' (fig. 18).[33]

Repton returned to Moggerhanger in 1795, perhaps just in passing, and his visit precipitated a spate of works, including the building of Soane's picturesque entrance lodge and the planting of the related shelter belts and copses (which were all intact until after the end of the Second World War and the small copses flanking the gate on the Bedford road are still there). Further finishing touches, very typical Repton delights, included the 'Tudor cottage' beside the kitchen garden wall, which was perhaps an aviary, a menagerie and kennels, a filbert walk, an alcove seat and a rustic summerhouse.

The following year, 1796, he came again to deal with the important southward view over Beeston Leasows. He suggested removal of some hedges to smooth the profile of the fields, and that a cottage in the view could be painted prettily with green doors and windows and planted with flowers so 'that it may not appear the humble habitation of a poor Labourer but rather the reward of some favourite Servant, made comfortable by the elegant attention of the Ladies, who may be supposed

fig. 18 Repton's idea illustrated in the 1792 'Mogenhanger' Red Book was that a viewpoint should be a surprise on a walk through the woods, as this view to the east and the Everton ridge, the reverse of fig. 15.

to take pleasure in decorating this little Spot'.[34] Green paint was the most expensive and thus spoke of fashion, and this little exercise in rural art was the acme of gentility.

In Repton's career Moggerhanger was the sweet filling in a substantially encrusted ducal sandwich: he worked at Welbeck for the Duke of Portland immediately before and just after Moggerhanger, and soon afterwards he was taken up by the 6th Duke of Bedford for his famous commissions at Woburn and at Endsleigh in Devon. It was unlikely that he appeared at Moggerhanger again, but his far-seeing genius had supplied the blueprint for an enchantingly Reptonian setting, and his grumbles about the shortcomings of the place were to be remembered and repaired.

Humphry Repton (fig. 19) and John Soane had several clients in common and their paths often crossed, but it cannot be said that they were friends. Soane really liked to have architectural control over the landscape settings of his houses and much preferred working with an amenable gardener – as he did with John Haverfield at Tyringham – than tangling with the critical Repton.[35] Repton in his turn found Soane eccentric, even perverse in his search for 'novelty', but was 'delighted with the animation of his manner' and would like to have known him better; pursuing this end Repton attended a Soane lecture at the Royal Academy, only to hear himself 'abused and held up to ridicule'.

Repton went up to Soane, they shook hands and enjoyed more 'sparring with buttons on, and our sharp play does not matter a button,' was their mutual verdict.[36]

Repton's jibes in his Red Book about Moggerhanger wanting 'more importance of Character' and the low sills of the arched windows making both Eating and Drawing Rooms vulnerable to the 'defilement' of the waiting carriage horses, nettled Soane, and brought him speeding to Moggerhanger on the mail coach *Highflier* in June 1797 to discuss changes with Godfrey Thornton. Ideas included an oval breakfast room in the centre of the south front, a single-storey pavilion on the south-west corner for a breakfast room and a big extension westwards into the stable yard. The east entrance portico was to be unchanged. Did Soane really know that this was the key to the problems; did Godfrey Thornton refuse to countenance any disturbance to Mrs Thornton's dressing room? Whatever the difficulties, nothing happened, except some freshening of the outside paintwork and interior decorations.

fig. 19 Humphry Repton 1752–1818, coined the term 'landscape gardener'.

It was equally feasible that outside factors delayed any changes. Godfrey Thornton was sixty in 1797, he had served his term as Governor of the Bank of England and earned all the plaudits that the City of London can bestow, and yet there was no sign of his permanent retirement to the country. His architect too was busy,[37] and Soane's new Bank of England was emerging from the shell of the old, a fortress filled with caves of light: the Stock and Dividend offices, the Rotunda, the Bullion gate and Lothbury court – soon to be followed by the Governor's court. It was a fortress against a city, and country, in turmoil (fig. 20). There was a catastrophic run on the Bank in February 1797 with stocks 'falling to a record low and £100,000 a day being withdrawn'. The febrile mood lurched from gloom to euphoria – joy at Nelson's victories at Cape St Vincent (February 1797) and at Aboukir Bay (summer 1798) – to despair at news of the naval mutiny, rebellion in Ireland and Napoleon's victory at Marengo (June 1800). William Pitt, who had materially shored up the national defences, bowed to political pettinesses at home and resigned in the spring of 1801. Nelson's victory at Copenhagen was cheered in June, but the now annual summer panic that the 'Frenchies' were

fig. 20 James Gillray, *The Bank Picquet* 1787 satirising the intimidating tactics of the Bank of England's guards.

coming was bolstered by reports of Napoleon's invasion camps being readied all along the Channel coast. Soane's Bank became a symbol of the proverbial British bulldog at bay. It was certainly central to his own career, occupying 'pride of place in his self-appreciation as an architect'[38] and he could have had little doubt that his clients and friends at the Bank, led by Godfrey Thornton, had made this possible.

Godfrey Thornton was appointed as High Sheriff for Bedfordshire in 1803 and settled at Moggerhanger at last. Was he relieved to be well out of the City's most severe invasion fever the following New Year, when it was mooted that the court were to flee to Worcester and the Bank's gold was all to be stored in the Cathedral there? He preferred to go to Woburn for the duke's first sheepshearing that spring of 1804, where he enjoyed the society of farmers and countrymen. But it was not to be for long, for Godfrey Thornton died on the 5 November 1805, aged sixty-nine, and the news of his death was carried in the same London papers as the fortnight-old news of Admiral Nelson's victory and death at the battle of Trafalgar. Godfrey Thornton was mourned by his wife and family who placed his memorial in Blunham church 'to commemorate the virtues of an excellent man' and 'most kind parent'. Jane Thornton lived until 5 March 1811, aged sixty-seven, when she too was buried in the Blunham vault.

CLAPHAM POSTSCRIPT

At Clapham Godfrey's cousin, John Thornton – immensely rich, spectacularly philanthropic but *rough* – had died in 1790, to be succeeded by his three sons, Samuel, Robert and Henry in both fortunes and beliefs. It was Henry Thornton (1760–1815), a banker at Down, Thornton & Free, and close friend and fellow Member of the House of Commons with William Wilberforce, who masterminded 'the colony of heaven' which came to be called the Clapham Sect. Henry Thornton bought a house called 'Battersea Rise', building villas in the grounds for his friends Charles Grant and Edward Eliot. The latter was William Pitt's brother-in-law, a sorrowing young widower with a small daughter, and Pitt came often to see them, hence Battersea Rise became associated with both the Clapham 'Saints' and Pitt's circle. William Pitt, like his father the Earl of Chatham, was passionately interested in building and gardening. Pitt proposed the design of an oval library for Battersea Rise, at the same time as Soane was designing an oval breakfast room for Moggerhanger.

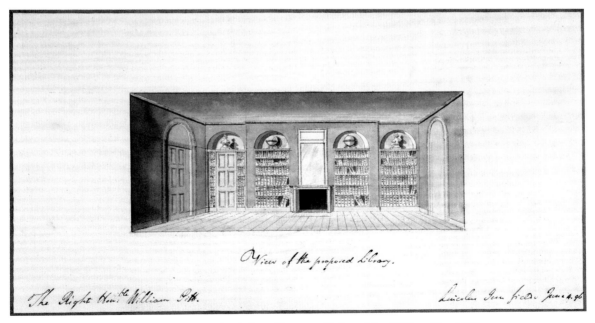

fig. 21 John Soane, sketch for a library at Holwood for William Pitt, 1796.

fig. 22 Moggerhanger House, Mrs Thornton's Dressing Room as in 2012 (after restoration).

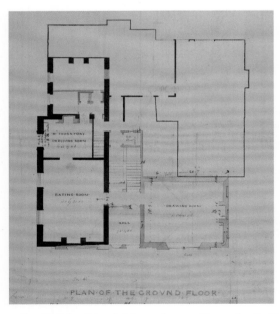
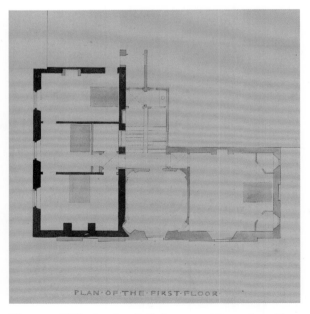

fig. 23 John Soane's Moggerhanger House for Godfrey Thornton 1791, showing (left) the ground floor plan with the small entrance hall on the east front, and Mr Thornton's room on the south front, and (right) the first floor with the curving walls of Mrs Thornton's Dressing Room over the east entrance, this room surviving all subsequent alterations.

He had also designed a library for Pitt's country house Holwood in Kent (fig. 21). It is easy to imagine that the architect was a great deal 'put upon'; but, says Gillian Darley, Soane was 'determinedly professional' in soliciting Pitt's patronage and always restrained.[39] Repton, on the other hand, claimed to have stayed overnight at Holwood, and that he and Pitt explored the woods by moonlight, planning vistas of the Kent countryside.

It was in that oval library at Battersea Rise that the Clapham Sect resolved their good works, supporting Hannah More's schools,[40] deciding to publish the *Christian Observer* and a stream of tracts and sermons. They formalised old John Thornton's distribution of bibles into the British and Foreign Bible Society in 1804, which led to the founding of the Church Missionary Society. In the library there was talk of Trafalgar, of Nelson's state funeral on 9 January 1806, and then, just a fortnight later, shock and sorrow at the news of Pitt's death at the age of forty-six, worn out from work and worry over the Allied defeat at Austerlitz. But the following year brought a famous victory with the vote for Britain's abolition of the slave trade. Henry Thornton, 'pious, benevolent, serious, shrewd',[41] had been particularly close to Godfrey Thornton, with whom he had served his banking apprenticeship. It can be surmised that Godfrey, though no radical, played his part in interesting Henry Thornton in the bad practices of the slave trade, which led Henry, Wilberforce and Thomas Clarkson and their friends to force the famous vote for abolition in 1807.

STEPHEN THORNTON AND JOHN SOANE

Stephen Thornton (1767–1850) inherited, at the age of thirty-eight, the Moggerhanger estate at his father's death. He enjoyed what by now seemed the Thornton fiefdoms: a commission in the Grenadier Guards, the family businesses, a director's chair at the Bank of England, and other enterprises which included a hand in the development of the London docks. In 1794 Stephen had married Mary Littledale, who had been brought up in Rotterdam where her father was in business. Mary and Stephen lived in fashionable Harley Street, rearing an ever-increasing family – eventually ten sons and a single daughter – and so a country house was a timely inheritance (figs. 24 and 25).

The Park house was clearly much too small for these younger Thorntons, and so John Soane was sent for again. Repton's Red Book was also to hand, and his unhappy remarks about the inadequacy of the house for its position, for 'such a command of property', and the 'difficulty in the management' of the views from the drawing room windows were clearly all discussed. John Soane, it must be added, was at the height of his fame and ingenuity when he returned to Moggerhanger in 1806: he and Eliza and the family now lived at 12 Lincoln's Inn Fields, which he had rebuilt in his own manner, he had bought and was rebuilding Pitzhanger Manor at Ealing as a country home, he had a royal appointment as Clerk of Works at St James's Palace and the Houses of Parliament, had been elected a Royal Academician and, in the early spring of 1806, Professor of Architecture at the Academy.[42]

He had developed a remarkably facility for 'juggling' the interior spaces of a building's envelope and his ingenuity was endless. In January 1807 he sent Stephen Thornton an exquisite

fig. 24 Stephen Thornton (1767–1850)
by Henry Wyatt.

fig. 25 Stephen's wife Mary, née Littledale,
and four of her children by Daniel Gardner.

perspective of a possible house, the classical entrance portico with Mrs Thornton's dressing room balcony retained on the east front (keeping the upstairs dressing room as its charming self was undoubtedly a proviso), but with the principal reception rooms in line along the south front. The drawing room, a bow-windowed breakfast room and the Eating Room all had the lovely views over seemingly endless woods and hills. The entrance vestibule was low, classically Greek Doric with fluted columns, tunnelling into the centre of the house and bursting out into a light and airy stair hall. The north wing was to have a library (next to the front door), a small oval business room for Stephen Thornton, and the housekeeper's room.

Soane, in his thorough way, then proposed a resurvey of the house in 1808; his characteristic way of working was to produce varied schemes and 'keep cogitating'. This brought him the realisation that it was the entrance on the *east* front that was the limiting factor, and so he decided to *turn the house around again*, making the entrance on the *north side*. This 'north entrance and staircase hall at the core of the building,' says Peter Inskip, 'shifted the centre of gravity and provided a much more cohesive plan, allowing the principal rooms to wrap around the centre of gravity'.[43] He gave Stephen

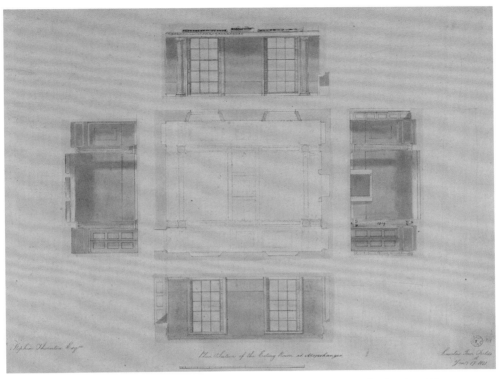

fig. 26 John Soane, Plan and internal elevations of the Eating Room for Stephen Thornton,
January 1811, showing the increasing refinement of Moggerhanger's design.

Thornton three options for his new north entrance front, which resulted, in June 1809, in an elegantly drawn elevation showing the single-storey Entrance Hall, how the first floor was cut back, and the third floor was a low central tower with a balustrade around its roof.[44]

Stephen Thornton seems to have been a softer man than his father. He was confident and urbane, thoroughly at home in the country, delighted with Soane's ideas, and in turn Soane warmed to him as a client. This good relationship resulted in the 'campaign' of rebuilding between 1810 and 1812 which changed Moggerhanger into a substantial country house – a 'design so gradually refined so that eventually the judicious massing of the house gave the impression of a building far larger than it was in reality'.[45]

The works were extensive; the roof was taken off, the attic storey removed, the western half of the house demolished and rebuilt on a much larger scale, removing the staircase and kitchen offices originally built for Godfrey Thornton in 1792. The eastern section, the old east entrance hall, the drawing room below Mrs Thornton's dressing room and the Eating Room with bedroom above were remodelled externally to bring all into line with the new work (fig. 26). However, Mrs Thornton's

fig. 27 Moggerhanger House 2006, the north and east fronts after restoration,
photographed by June Buck for *Country Life*.

dressing room, now known as the 'boudoir', was little changed – it was, in fact, preserved intact. The new mansard roof, covered in Westmorland slating, was a very fashionable French touch and considerably in advance of the mansard-roofed Wrest Park of 1834–6.

The new north front (fig. 27) sported ornaments and allusions that Soane realised would be appreciated. The portico had six fluted Doric columns, their flutings echoing the latest archaeological discoveries in the Ancient World;[46] the arched windows, some dummies for symmetry's sake, were a feature of the façade, with especially wide windows for each of the rooms (library to the left, housekeeper's to the right) in the wings which projected forwards beneath shallow pediments, rather as seen on Roman tombs. The balustrade to the first floor and tower had balusters of Coade stone, delivered in December 1809. The stone finishings are all of Ketton limestone, from the quarry outside Stamford. The main surface finish was rendered in Parker's Metallic Stucco to match the original work on Godfrey Thornton's house, and limewashed, though now, in 1810, in a stronger ochre or straw colouring.

Moggerhanger's east front was now free to be a garden façade, and Soane gave this a delicate two-storeyed verandah, which served Mr Thornton's room on the ground floor and the boudoir above. The drawing room, breakfast room and Eating Room were ranged along the south front, with huge rectangular windows opening on to the views over Beeston Leasows. The service wing had been pushed progressively westwards each time that Moggerhanger was enlarged. Now Soane designed a new kitchen pavilion, with attendant sculleries – the main scullery had piped water and sink soakaways in 1811 – a china closet, pantry and servants' hall. This Servants' Hall 'was a

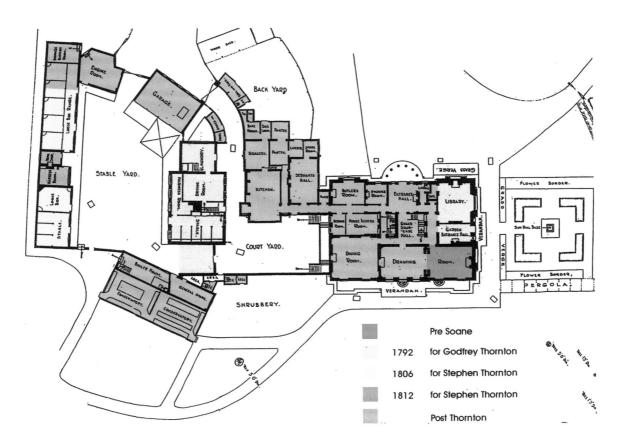

Pre Soane

1792   for Godfrey Thornton

1806   for Stephen Thornton

1812   for Stephen Thornton

Post Thornton

fig. 28 Peter Inskip, Inskip + Jenkins' plan to show the stages of construction that survive, only half the drawing room from the old Muggerhanger Lodge, and the bulk of the fabric remaining from Soane's major rebuilding for Stephen Thornton, which influenced the date for the restoration – to 1812.

handsome, symmetrical space with arched recesses either side of the fireplace' and a large tripartite sash window looking out to the Portico. The old stables were converted into a laundry and drying room, and further west still was the newer Stable Court. The piped water was pumped from the well by a William Good horse-power engine (parts of which survive in the engine house) up to storage tanks in the tower and thence to a water closet (WC) in the entrance hall and another upstairs, but otherwise only the scullery and the housekeeper's room. There was still a deal of carrying ewers, jugs and buckets to be done by the maids, but at least this whole new service wing – with smooth stone floors and stone colour-washed walls – was light and airy, and comparatively easy to keep clean.

As the final touches were being added to the new Moggerhanger in 1812–13 it becomes clear that Stephen Thornton had complete confidence in his architect, and that Soane was masterminding the entire concept. He organised the adjustments to the drives and walks for the north entrance portico and the extended stable wing to the west. The Moggerhanger Bill Books kept by the architect show that he supplied the Thorntons' every smallest need, sending a mason, bricklayer, glazier or painter whenever wanted. In 1812 these bills show the workmen doing odd repair jobs in the house but that their attentions were gradually drawn to the head gardener's establishment. This is revealed as the fully fledged *Victorian* garden rather before its time, with a pine house, pits for the pineapples, a peach house, greenhouse, fruit room, cucumber frames, a tool room, the gardeners' room where the men and boys would take their meals, and a stable for the horse which pulled the garden carts and the lawn-mowing machine.

John Soane had given Stephen Thornton and his family the most enchanting country house. In terms of colour and light this was a progress from the half-shade of the columned entrance portico into the richly oak-grained Entrance Hall, the atmosphere glowing with substance and assurance. To pass through the door into the staircase hall was to burst into the airy space, light tumbling from above, with the seemingly unsupported stair floating and curving upwards. All was painted in soft pink and dove grey, pink walls, grey woodwork, the theme of the core of the house, which quietened the mind.

The (central) drawing room did not seek to surprise except for the magnificent view through its tall windows, hung with heavy, rich curtains; this was now an elegant room, subtly rounded, with coolly violet walls and grey woodwork. As General Tilney in *Northanger Abbey* looked 'upon a tolerably large eating-room as one of the necessaries of life'[47] so did Stephen Thornton. In the Eating Room Soane had moved the Ionic columns – which conventionally shelter the sideboards – from the ends of the room and reused them for screens at the sides, emphasising the focus on the dining table.

Upstairs, all pink walls and soft grey woodwork, one can hear the Austen heroines all gasping in delight at the boudoir, the ladies' retiring room. This exotic room, Soane's first work retained all through subsequent changes, with its ceiling painted with rosaries and ribbons, ice-cream colours, simple white marble chimneypiece and balcony view, retained its feminine enchantment in what was, after all, a house of masculine values.

We know that after Wellington's victory at Waterloo in 1815 England settled down to peace. In Bedfordshire the coronation of George IV in 1821 was celebrated in splendid style – the Rev.

Beachcroft, vicar at Blunham, noted that a 'quartern' loaf and 3lbs of meat, virtually a week's supply, were handed out in Moggerhanger parish, and that he, his mother Mrs Campbell and the Stephen Thorntons had been to a service and banquet at Biggleswade, with dancing on the lawn at Moggerhanger Park in the evening.[48]

The only other postscript to Soane's work at Moggerhanger comes from some letters that he kept. In December 1833 it seemed that the impossible was happening: Stephen Thornton was short of money, and had been borrowing from his architect. He wrote asking for an extension of a loan for £500 for another six months, adding that he would call at Lincoln's Inn Fields just two days before Christmas to pay the interest. The architect, now Sir John and very rich, was also known to be kind and generous to his friends; the following June (1834) Stephen Thornton was again extending his loan. We know no more. Except that the following year there was a great Whit Sunday storm at Moggerhanger with hailstones big enough to break the glasses in the hothouses and greenhouse: by August they had counted up sixteen toplights and thirty-two sliding lights broken in the greenhouse, which had to be repaired for the autumn, and 1,030 broken panes in the four hothouses. It seems that the faithful William Watson, who had done so much of the painting and glazing well over twenty years' earlier, came to Stephen Thornton's rescue.[49]

Stephen Thornton died at Moggerhanger on 26 August 1850 at the grand old age of eighty-three; he was buried in the vault at Blunham, with his wife Mary, who had died four years' earlier, aged seventy-one. Sadly the memorials at Blunham show that four of their ten sons died in childhood. Their heir Godfrey's young first wife, Susanna Dixon, is also buried there. This Godfrey, formerly a colonel in the Grenadier Guards, married secondly Sophia Pearse, but only briefly enjoyed his Moggerhanger inheritance as he died only seven years after his father, in March 1857, aged sixty-one.

On a lighter note, Stephen and Mary's eighth son, Colonel William Thornton (1808–64), had bought the land belonging to Samuel Sutton (the second of that name, known as Sam Sutton, gent., 'of Moggerhanger') after his death in 1848, and built his own house at the end of Moggerhanger village, calling it St John's. His grandson thought that the name 'St John's' came from Colonel William's service with the Grenadiers in St John's, Newfoundland; if so, it is a colourful story – the Guards were sent there in 1839 to deal with a French uprising, a campaign remembered for Jacob the Goose giving the alarm on a snowy night, which saved many lives in the face of a rebel attack. The battalion brought Jacob home, an honoured member of the regiment, a happy ending until he was knocked down and killed by a van in a London street. Jacob's stuffed head still finds a place in the Guards' Museum at Wellington Barracks.

VICTORIAN AND EDWARDIAN MOGGERHANGER
Stephen Thornton had lived to such a great age that it was natural that his children had establishments of their own. Sophia Pearse after the death of her husband, Godfrey, lived at her family home at Woodford in Essex, and their daughter Mary was married to Charles Pearse and they

THIRD EDITION.

BEDFORDSHIRE.

Particulars

OF

HIGHLY DESIRABLE AND IMPORTANT

FREEHOLD ESTATES,

KNOWN AS

MOGGERHANGER AND BEESTON,

SITUATE IN THE PARISHES OF

BLUNHAM, NORTHILL, SANDY, AND GREAT BARFORD,

IN A PICTURESQUE AND FERTILE PART OF THE

COUNTY OF BEDFORD,

About 3 miles from Sandy, 5 miles from Bedford, and within 48 miles of London.

CONSISTING OF A

COMMODIOUS FAMILY MANSION,

CALLED

MOGGERHANGER HOUSE,

SITUATE IN A RICHLY-TIMBERED PARK;

WITH

Offices, Gardens and Pleasure Grounds, Several Capital Farms and Homesteads,

A WATER CORN-MILL,

"THE GUINEA" AND "BEESTON CROSS" PUBLIC HOUSES,

NUMEROUS LABORERS' COTTAGES & ENCLOSURES OF ACCOMMODATION & MARKET GARDEN LAND,

TOGETHER WITH

THE MANORS AND FISHERIES,

THE WHOLE INCLUDING

2056a. 3r. 33p.

OF

MOST FERTILE LAND,

Which will be Sold by Auction, by

MESSRS.

BEADEL AND SONS,

AT THE AUCTION MART, BARTHOLOMEW LANE, LONDON,

On TUESDAY, the 4th day of AUGUST, 1857,

At Twelve o'Clock, in Twenty-nine Lots.

Particulars, with Lithographic Plan, may be obtained of Messrs. ANDERSON & SHOUBRIDGE, Solicitors, 1, Lincoln's Inn Fields; Messrs. C. J. & H. WILSHAW, Solicitors, 3, Gray's Inn Square; of Mr. STAFFORD, Bedford; at the Auction Mart; and of Messrs. BEADEL & SONS, 25, Gresham Street, London, E.C., of whom alone Orders to View may be obtained.

fig. 29 Beadel and Sons sale advertised for 4th August 1857 of the estate of over 2,000 acres and all the buildings and properties that the Thorntons had amassed in just over one hundred years.

lived in Oxfordshire. Of Stephen's surviving sons Colonel William was at St John's, Harry Thornton and his family were at Kempston Grange and the Rev. George Thornton was at Beeston Leasows Farm. Additional land in Northill parish was held in trust for the heirs of the fifth son Stephen Edward. Stephen Thornton's surviving brother, Claude George, and his wife, Frances, had long enjoyed their own Soane house, Marden Hill in Hertfordshire.[50]

So, after the death of Colonel Godfrey Thornton in 1857 the Moggerhanger (Park) house and estate were surplus to family requirements, and duly prepared for sale. The Moggerhanger and Beeston estates were offered for sale by auction by Messrs Beadel and Sons of Bartholomew Lane, London, on the 4 August 1857 (fig. 29). The sale particulars give details of the legacy that Godfrey and Stephen Thornton had created: the estate extended just over 2,056 acres, and included The

ONE

Guinea and Beeston Cross public houses, the Park Farm (284 acres, tenancy with the Brown family, William Brown) and Willow Hill Farm (235 acres, tenancy Benjamin Brown), the farms at Chalton, Budna and South Mills, the corn mill at South Mills, fishing rights on the Ouse and Ivel, a great deal of fertile market garden land and the picturesque estate houses and cottages. The principal lot (of twenty-nine in all) was naturally the 'Commodious Family Mansion' – 'in perfect order and (except for the Drawing Room and Music Room which require decorating) fit for the immediate occupation of a Family of distinction' – set in just over a thousand acres of richly timbered parkland.

The 'Mansion' had acquired all the trappings of a Victorian country house; Soane's carefully named Eating Room was now the 'dining room', the communicating doors between the music room and drawing room could be folded back for parties and country dances, there was a 'Fire-proof Strong Room' and a hat room. The housekeeper's room, butler's pantry, servants' hall, footmen's room and the 'large and lofty kitchen' were all in excellent order, with additional rooms in the cellar for (travelling bags and) Boxes, (sharpening) Knives and (polishing) Boots – all the paraphernalia of the Victorian country house, along with the 'extensive Wine, Beer and Coal Cellarage'. Upstairs there were four large bedrooms with dressing rooms – including Mrs Thornton's still 'elegant' boudoir – and nursery quarters; on the third floor were eleven smaller rooms, carefully detailed by Soane, each with a fireplace, and intended for visiting bachelors and resident and visiting maids, the conventional but hazardous arrangement in any less than well-run household. The male staff slept over the kitchen court, laundry and wash houses; there were four grooms' rooms, stabling for thirteen horses, four single coach houses and standing for four more carriages.

The chief feature of the garden is the 'Handsome Newly-Erected Conservatory'; lawns, flower gardens and shrub borders surround the house, and 'delightful walks through thriving groves and Plantations lead to the Rustic Summer House' and the ice house. The orchard and kitchen gardens 'enclosed and divided by lofty walls' with their full complement of potting sheds, tool houses and forcing grounds were all in working and fruiting order.[51]

Once again there is something of a mystery as to why the estate was put up for auction in August 1857 as a buyer had already been found by Mary Pearse. The sellers were actually Stephen and Mary Thornton's ninth son, Harry, of Kempston Grange and his nephew-in-law, Charles Pearse, and the buyers were the Rev. Edward Henry Dawkins (1794–1859) of Over Norton in Oxfordshire and his wife, Elizabeth, or rather their trustees. Elizabeth Dawkins was an heiress by virtue of the death of her mother Dame Isabella Bell Cooper on 27 January 1855, leaving a fortune of some £30,000 from property in London and the West Indies, to be spent on buying an English home. The Rev. Edward Dawkins had a timely inheritance, in 1857, of a collection of fine paintings from his cousin Caroline Dawkins and was in need of a suitable house in which to hang them.[52] The private sale was agreed on 19 February 1858, but Edward Dawkins did not have long to enjoy his house or the pictures for he died just over a year later, on 18 May 1859. Moggerhanger was left in trust for Edward and Elizabeth's son, Edward Henry Frederick Dawkins (1837–1912), who married that year, 1859, Louisa Barnett of Stratton Park (figs. 30, 31 and 32).

figs. 30, 31 and 32 From left to right, Mrs Elizabeth Dawkins who built Moggerhanger's church, her son Edward Henry Frederick Dawkins and his wife Louisa, née Barnett of Stratton Park.

fig. 33 St John the Evangelist, Moggerhanger, from an old postcard, 1907.

Moggerhanger was accorded the status of an ecclesiastical parish in 1860, and Elizabeth Dawkins paid for the building of St John the Evangelist Church in beautifully crafted local stones with oak for the roof from the estate and glass by Clayton & Bell (fig. 33). The church and the adjacent vicarage were built by Mr Conquest of Kempston to the designs of William Slater (who also worked on the churches at Winwick and Brington in east Huntingdonshire). The church, consecrated on 31 July 1861, was Elizabeth's memorial to her husband, and she also paid for a village school which formerly stood on the site of the present village hall. Sadly this beneficent lady died only two years after completion of the church, on 8 September 1863, and so it remains her memorial as well.

The Moggerhanger estate – or Morhanger as the Dawkins preferred to call it – remained the home of Edward Henry Frederick and Louisa Dawkins, their two sons and their daughter, Ethel Louise (1868–1954), for another twenty-two years. There is every indication that the Dawkins family were excellent owners, they kept the house in splendid condition and encouraged 'a prosperous and contented tenantry' through good years. Most evidently they were keen gardeners, planting many exotic trees and shrubs around the house, very much in the fashion of the times – the copper beech, cedar of Lebanon, *Cedrus deodara*, *Araucaria imbricata* (monkey puzzle), pines, magnolias, cherries, maples and the *Sequoiadendron giganteum*, the *Wellingtonia*, only introduced to England in 1853, were all their plantings. They planted a Filbert Walk which led beneath elm shade to a sunny Rosary – a circular pattern of beds usually surrounded by a trellis – with 100 varieties of dwarf and standard roses.

The kitchen gardens were fully maintained and continued to be productive with an emphasis on the production of soft and wall fruit. It was a matter of pride that the Ice House was so well shaded that it only needed filling once a year – and shade was also a benefit to the ladies' complexions for it was equally pleasant that the Summer House afforded 'charming views' over the park and distant hills, and yet 'during the hottest summers, the rays of (the) sun seldom penetrate'. For tennis parties four Lawn Courts were made and maintained on the east side of the house, these partly screened by a long herbaceous border (fig. 34).

In 1873 a timely survey of Bedfordshire estates[53] showed the domination of the 9th Duke of Bedford with 33,500 acres, all farmed by the most modern methods, at Woburn, followed by the equally pioneering Samuel Whitbread with just over 13,000 acres at Southill. The Dawkins' Morhanger was well down the list with other gentlemen's agricultural and sporting estates of around 2,000 acres. Just five years later, in 1878, Queen Victoria was informed by her Prime Minister, Benjamin Disraeli, Lord Beaconsfield, that 'the Duke of Bedford is the wealthiest of Your Majesty's subjects; his income absolutely exceeding £300,000 a year'.[54] The duke had his London Bloomsbury estates to shore up his income but for most of Britain's farmers and estate owners relying on their rentals, catastrophe was on hand. Once again, a century after the bad harvests that marred Godfrey Thornton's arrival at Moggerhanger, the cycle was repeated. The summer of 1879 was a fifth consecutively wet season, the ever-increasing imports of cheap American wheat depressed prices for what could be grown, and there were annual outbreaks of animal diseases, culminating in an epidemic of foot and mouth in

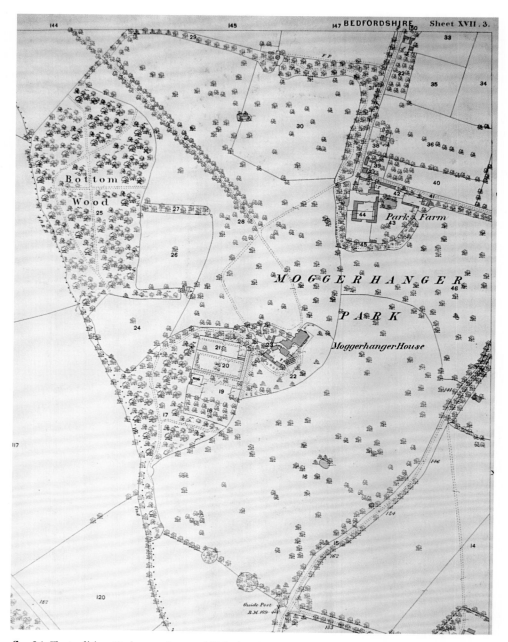

fig. 34 First edition Ordnance Survey 1885, showing how well Repton's recommended planting has matured; the Entrance lodge survives at the top of the map, but a new straight drive has been made directly and farther west onto the Bedford road. The survey does not show the formal gardens and tennis lawns laid out on the east front of the house which were thought to be made by E.H.F. Dawkins and his wife Louisa, who were keen gardeners.

cattle in 1883.[55] Land went out of cultivation, the people who had worked it left for the towns, the awful British agricultural depression of the 1880s had arrived.

Once again it became all too clear that fortunes do not last, that Edward Henry Frederick Dawkins had been raising mortgages on his estate among his trustees, and so once again it was prepared for sale, this time in 1885. It was to be marketed to new money fortunates by Messrs Walton and Lee of Tokenhouse Yard in the City of London, on Thursday, 24 September 1885 (fig. 35), at 2 o'clock 'precisely', with the emphasis on 'a very valuable and highly attractive Freehold Residential and Sporting Estate with an elegant mansion, and 1,314 or so acres producing some £2,492 a year in rentals'. The sale particulars were a sumptuous document, with at least twenty different decorative typefaces rippling down the pages to attract attention to the portico's 'six massive stone columns, the beautiful grand hall, the principal staircase of solid stone with polished hand rail', the handsome gallery on the first floor, the boudoir and blue, green and pink bedrooms, the pleasant domestic offices, the copious stabling and 'capital' dog kennels. However, it was indicative of Sir John Soane's reputation, in the doldrums at just short of fifty years after his death, that the house was trumpeted as 'in the Grecian style from designs by Inigo Jones'.

Once again Moggerhanger did not fall prey to the open market, for there was to be no strange new owner. Edward Henry Frederick Dawkins moved to Northamptonshire, leaving Morhanger Park, as it was now conventionally called, occupied by Richard Mercer (1825–1904) of East Farleigh, the Dawkins' chief trustee. At his death it passed to his son Colonel Algernon Mercer (with interests held by his brothers, Randall Mercer of Sandling Park and Herbert Mercer, colonel of the 3rd Dragoons, based at The Curragh in County Kildare, and other trustees). In the early years of the twentieth century the Mercers negotiated a private sale of the estate, yet again to someone they

knew, a fellow (military) and sporting gentleman, kinsman of the Earl of Westmorland, Sydney Algernon Fane (1867–1929). The sale was completed on 30 October 1907 in the name of Mrs Fane (fig. 36), the former Selina Violet Fitzwygram, and her trustees. The Fanes had been married for thirteen years and they had four sons, Aubrey aged twelve, Gerard aged nine, Kenneth five and the baby Nigel, three years' old (fig. 38). Sydney Fane's claim to distinction was as Master of the South Oxfordshire Foxhounds, (fig. 37) so we may assume that his sons had an energetic

fig. 35 Moggerhanger Park house, engraving of the entrance front from the Sale Particulars of 24th September 1885.

From top left clockwise:
fig. 36 Mrs Selina Violet Fane, the 'lady of the Manor' from 1907 until 1914.
fig. 37 Sydney Algernon Fane 1867–1929 as Master of the South Oxfordshire Hunt.
fig. 38 The four sons of Sydney and Selina Fane in the East garden – from right to left, Aubrey, Gerard, Kenneth and Nigel.

outdoor upbringing at Moggerhanger. Selina Fane was regarded as the 'lady of the manor'; she made some necessary repairs and additions to the house (rainwater heads bear the date 1908) and she was the most likely creator of the formal flower gardens on the east front, below her boudoir balcony. The Fanes had only seven short years to enjoy their country home before the declaration of war in August 1914. Aubrey and Gerard Fane both volunteered, and both survived the war, but the family left Moggerhanger for London and Mrs Fane lived in Dover Street, off Piccadilly; she died in 1939.

With the outbreak of war in 1914 Moggerhanger Park, along with almost every other country house of any size, became subject to the laws of requisition for emergency uses; for four years it was home to the evacuated staff and pupils of Godwin College from Harold Road, Cliftonville at Margate. Margate was then famous for having more schools and colleges than any other town in Britain, all prospering on healthy regimes of sea bathing, fresh air and exercise and 'most liberal diets', but now a prey to the anxieties of nervous parents because of its strategic position on the Kent coast. Godwin College – which prepared boys 'for Commercial and Professional Life' and claimed the 'Highest Successes in Examinations' – normally occupied a pair of red brick and tile-hung houses in the Arts and Crafts style in a quiet road off Cliftonville Esplanade and close to the Walpole Rocks Bathing Pool. The Girls' College was further along the sea front at Palm Bay (and this building survives as Godwin Court flats). The College left Moggerhanger in the spring of 1919.[56]

In 1917 Mrs Fane's mortgages on the estate were returned to her so that it could be put on the market yet again, to be sold by auction at the Red Lion Hotel in Sandy by F. W. Western on 21 March. It was still 'Morhanger Park'. The house and pleasure grounds of just over twenty-seven acres were Lot 1; Park Farm was Lot 2, with twenty-seven additional lots of market garden or smallholding lands. Remarkably the surveyed plan of the smallholding lots shows that Repton's plantings all along the park boundaries were intact. Lot 1 was reserved (pending the County Council's decision to purchase it), but Lot 2 was bought by a local businessman, Mr Frank Odell of Market Square, Sandy, for £15,000, and remained his property until his death in 1946. Frank Odell and his sons Leslie and Ronald were market gardeners, and they managed these smallholdings for almost thirty years (fig. 39). Moggerhanger had gone back to its roots – literally, for John Byng had noted the sandy fields cropped with carrots, cucumbers, peas, parsnips and beans, as they had been since the seventeenth century, for half the residents of Sandy were market gardeners.

THE PARK HOSPITAL 1919–1987

When Godwin College left in 1919 the house was left empty, all the Fanes' furnishings were long gone and there was presumably some wear and tear on the elegant mansion from the passage of exuberant youth. Margate, it must be noted, was not only famous for healthily run schools and colleges but also for the Royal Sea Bathing Hospital, which was pioneering cures for many ills, most notably tuberculosis. It seems too much of a coincidence that Godwin College, forced to leave the fresh air of Margate, should find refuge in the high and airy inland Moggerhanger without someone

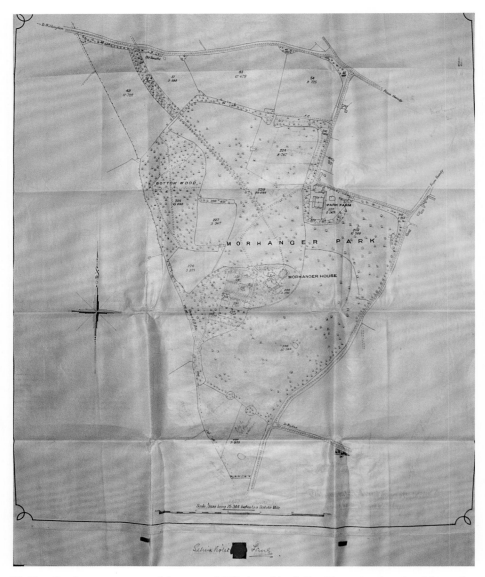

fig. 39 Plan for the conveyance of the estate 1917 signed by Selina Fane, showing that Moggerhanger Park survived intact until this moment, when for a sale advertised in March 1917 at the Red Lion Hotel, Sandy, it was divided into 28 Lots; Lot 1 was the house and Garden Wood (to Bedfordshire CC); Lot 2 was Park Farm and the adjoining paddock; 7 lots ranged along the southern (Beeston) boundary, another 7 through Bottom Wood and west of the drive to the Bedford road, and 6 along the Bedford road, another 5 in the inner park. These were to be market gardens.

making the connection? Was it the same connection that now worked its way through to Bedfordshire County Council, who had resolved to find a site for a county sanatorium in 1914.

It was not only in Bedfordshire but the whole national scheme for fighting the 'great white plague', tuberculosis of the lungs (consumption, phthisis, 'graveyard cough'), had been thrown into confusion with the declaration of war in 1914 with hospitals, sanitaria and nursing services diverted to the war effort. Despite medical advances, tuberculosis was then a terrible destroyer of young and active lives, attacking both men and women in their twenties and early thirties and especially those in certain occupations – workers with metals, stone and leather, printers, laundresses and even bakers being at risk – as well as those with their immunity lowered by a poor diet or emotional 'upset' (what we would call stress).[57] It was a disease of overcrowded town living, or perhaps of former country people unused to town conditions. It knew no social boundaries and was to be greatly aggravated by the armaments and war industries, let alone the ghastly conditions of the Western Front.

The national scheme was for a county-based network of local dispensaries for drugs, a sanatorium for early cases, outdoor schools and farm colonies, hospitals and after-care committees. In Bedfordshire, the County Council had identified Moggerhanger Park as suitable for a sanatorium, because of its high, free-draining and airy position, and it had been given a favourable medical assessment, but the project was 'reluctantly abandoned' in November 1914.[58]

By the time Godwin College left Moggerhanger in the spring of 1919 the need for a county sanatorium was urgent. Tuberculosis was the chief concern of the County Council's National Insurance Committee set up under Section 59 of Asquith and Lloyd George's National Insurance Act of 1911, by which all counties had to appoint a Tuberculosis Officer to whom all cases were reported, and who had to arrange for their treatment.[59] This 1911 Act, in which William Beveridge – later to be the architect of the National Health Service – played a part, was 'more comprehensive in its scope and more provident . . . in its machinery' than anything before it, so Asquith told George V.[60] The County Council were charged with the care of insured – and as it turned out uninsured – residents and discharged service personnel suffering from tuberculosis, who were entitled to residential treatment. Bedfordshire, with an entitlement to one bed in the Brompton Sanatorium at Frimley in Surrey, also sent cases to the Royal Sea Bathing Hospital at Margate and Northamptonshire Sanatorium at Creaton, but with cases rife in Luton and Bedford, the need for a local sanatorium was desperate. All methods of treatment were studied, including the Colony treatment at the Tuberculosis Colony established at Bourn, Cambridgeshire, in 1915, under the supervision of Dr Pendrill Varrier-Jones. The patients lived in somewhat Japanese-style wooden pavilions of their own making, with opening flaps which allowed them to sit in fresh air all day. Those that were fit enough worked at crafts or in the Colony garden.[61] The availability and advantages of Moggerhanger Park led to the decision for a county sanatorium.

The procedure to acquire Moggerhanger Park began on 28 November 1918 and on 5 February 1919 the NI Committee gave permission to start work on the planning of the Sanatorium and buying army huts 'of good construction'. On 14 February the *Biggleswade Chronicle* reported that the cost of

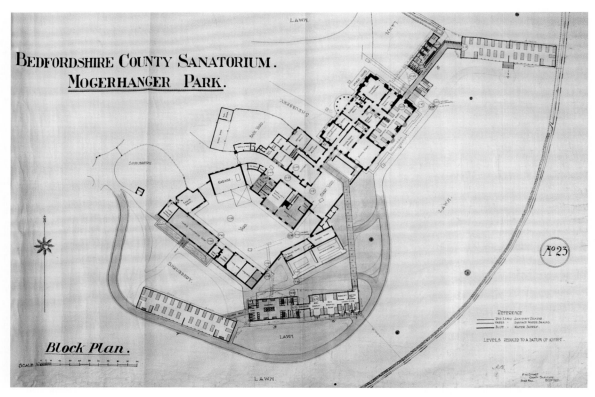

fig. 40 Bedfordshire County Sanatorium 1919, the County Architect's conversion of the ground floor to hospital use and including the placement of the pre-fabricated 'open-air' wards and the passages and paths made to serve them. Contrary to later perceptions of institutional use, this was initially a sensitive conversion.

At this stage little structural change was made to the house itself, partly for reasons of cost. The drawing room, with its large south-facing windows, became the women's ward for seriously ill patients, the Eating Room merely changed its name to the dining room, and other ground floor rooms were used for consulting and as a dispensary. The kitchen and former Servants' Hall remained the preserve of the staff, though this now included nursing staff. The kitchen court was now home to a large room full of washing machines and another for 'mangling and ironing'. Upstairs the bedrooms were used as children's wards and nurses' dormitories, and Matron occupied Mrs Thornton's Dressing Room. The attic rooms were used as additional staff accommodation.

Outside the hard-surface paths were necessary for trolleys and wheeled chairs to serve the additional pre-fabricated wards, three of which are shown on the east and south-west of the main house. There were also covered connecting ways. Bathroom and lavatory blocks were made in these pre-fabricated blocks to allow new drainage and supply pipes to be kept away from the more antiquated systems in the house. Bedfordshire County Council Architect's Department were well aware of the architectural quality of the house they were dealing with, at least up until the start of the war in 1939, but the transfer to the National Health Service after the war made more extreme alterations necessary.

the house was £7,000, additional accommodation would be in huts purchased from the Duke of Bedford's Military Camp in Ampthill Park at a cost of £1,400; sewage works were estimated at £1,600 and furnishing at £2,000. The Local Government Board would pay three-fifths of the total estimated cost of £12,000. On 21 November 1919 the County Council Clerk was authorised by the Ministry of Health to purchase the land and buildings at Moggerhanger Park 'for the purpose of a sanatorium for the treatment of TB'.[62] The Ministry had to see everything, especially the costs, and a long correspondence had followed, made difficult for a small council with only a skeleton staff, and the County Surveyor still on war service. The proposals were eventually submitted for Ministry approval on 6 December 1919, together with all the plans for the alterations to the house and the use of the long wooden wards, constructed for maximum fresh air, day and night, summer and winter. These wooden wards were connected to the main house by covered corridors; there were five, two extending from the east side, two on the south-west lawns beyond the conservatory and one on the north-west side. They were erected in the summer of 1919.

The surviving plans from the office of F.W. Smart, the County Surveyor, show just how the conversion of the house was carried out with great attention to detail and consideration for the character of Soane's work (fig. 40). In the dark days of the emergency situation of 1919 it is unlikely that the County Surveyor had access to Soane's drawings though they were still tucked away in 13 Lincoln's Inn Fields. In 1919 the house was surveyed – this 1919 survey being of great value to the architects of the present restoration. For the Sanatorium all three floors were fully utilised in housing the medical staff and children and women patients. The main works involved the installation of six bathrooms and additional WCs, far in excess of the usual standards of a country house. The conversion of Moggerhanger actually cost £20,344 – about £8,000 in excess of the early 1919 estimate. Tuberculosis was now so rife the government's allowances had been doubled, from £90 to £180 per head.[63]

Building works and the interior fitting-out were completed by the end of 1920. A gardener William Pettifer was appointed at thirty-five shillings per week, a cottage and his vegetables;[64] and a chauffeur/electrician Frederick Farnham at fifty shillings per week, with his cottage and vegetables. These rates were regularly raised, and additional gardeners employed. Right from the start it seems the kitchen gardens were maintained and readied to provide fresh vegetables and fruit for the hospital patients, and light work for those who felt able.

Seven candidates for the post of Matron were interviewed on 4 July 1921, and the post awarded to Miss Esther A. Winter from the Royal Berkshire Hospital at Reading. Her salary was £120 per annum rising to a maximum of £150; her assistant Miss E.E. Alderman was appointed in October at £70 per annum. The first patients arrived in January 1922. The county's NI Committee assessed each patient and listed their names and destinations in the huge red morocco-bound Minute Book. The majority were now sent to Moggerhanger. The Committee considered an average of twenty-five names at each meeting, a sad litany of lists, and yet not all were doomed and many were cured and sent out into the world again.

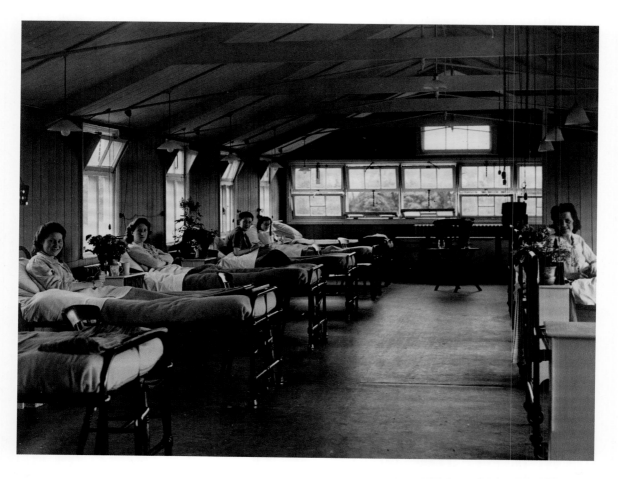

figs. 41 and 42 The Park Sanatorium served the people of Bedfordshire from 1922 until the late 1950s; these photographs taken in 1946 show one of the 'open-air' wards (above) and (below) Matron with County Officers, County Councillors and other staff members. The photograph may well indicate the end of an era, when the Sanatorium became part of the National Health Service.

Throughout the twenties and thirties there is every evidence that the Sanatorium was a highly regarded and hopeful place which settled into a well-managed routine. Gifts came in from all over the county: seed potatoes for the garden from a lady in Biddenham, regular baskets of fruit, a barrel of grapes, boxes of chocolates, a box of games, and, perhaps surprisingly to us, supplies of cigarettes from the British Red Cross. The paths around the house and through the garden were freshly gravelled; there was a difficulty over water quality and electric pumps and new tanks were installed in 1925. In May 1929, the County Medical Officer gave a summer house, one of the fashionable rotating pavilions easily turned for sun or shade. Every need was considered, were it for a new refrigerator, for curtains around the patients' beds to give added privacy or for changes in the bus service which brought visitors every Wednesday and Sunday. In the autumn, just before Christmas, there was always a concert party – Vauxhall Motors' Recreation Club Orchestra was often a star turn – and money was also always allowed for Christmas decorations. There were carol singers and we may be certain there was no shortage of presents and good food.

Throughout the 1920s and 1930s these Minute Books of the County Council's NI Committee[65] record a detailed picture of a forgotten world, our world before the National Health Service. Month by month the Committee went steadily on, reviewing each patient's means and the wherewithal of treating them either at Moggerhanger or elsewhere, recording these hundreds of private tragedies and joys.

The start of the Second World War in September 1939 hardly seemed to ruffle the Sanatorium's routine. Indeed, there appeared a small flag of defiance in the guise of an order for flowering trees and shrubs from the famous Wood & ingram's Nursery at Huntingdon; the ten items costing £4. 2s. 0d. included a crab apple, almond, cherry, laburnum and four scented lilacs and were sent by goods train to Sandy station. Simultaneously the nursery was packing a very similar order, though larger (just over £12), for Queen Elizabeth at Buckingham Palace – 'We'll gather lilacs in the spring again' being the morale-boosting refrain of the nation.[66]

However, after more than five years of privations and worries – over the increase in patients especially those from weapons' manufactories, over the difficulties of regular supplies of milk so vital for the patients and over the constant shortage of staff – the Park Hospital ran into difficulties. The summer of 1945 brought a flurry of special meetings to deal with complaints about the Sanatorium, about the food, the management, the isolation and even the treatment (figs. 41 and 42). Moggerhanger was not alone for official histories record that the whole sanatoria system was at 'near collapse' for want of staff. Eventually the Committee decided that it must 'deplore' the unwarranted agitation against the Santorium and its staff and ask the Resident Medical Officer and his colleagues to withdraw their resignations. The 'agitation' had come, it seemed, from the Bedford, Biggleswade and Luton Trades' Councils as a sharp squall from the approaching storm of post-war change; the war had been won, the people wanted a better world and they had voted in a Labour government proffering medical treatment for all 'free at the point of delivery'. Within three years the National Health Service was set up and the Park and Biggleswade Hospitals found themselves united in No. 1

Group, North-west Metropolitan Region managed by the Bedford Group Hospital Management Committee under the chairmanship of Major Simon Whitbread. A third tier, the Hospital House Committee, appointed in 1948 and re-appointed in 1958, ran the hospital much as before, but with a change in the treatment of tuberculosis (early diagnosis through regular chest X-rays and inoculation) the emphasis changed to treatment for the chronically sick and orthopaedic patients. In 1960 the Sanatorium connection ceased and it became Park Hospital and Rehabilitation Centre.

The house was still regularly repaired and redecorated, and hospital life was still cheered by visitors and entertainments. On 14 April 1966 the Committee's inspectors found the patients 'bright and cheery in spite of inclement weather' and in the gardens and greenhouses they were 'very impressed with the standard of work' – Moggerhanger's gardens supplied produce to the kitchens and to other hospitals in the group.

However, this pointed praise of the gardeners' work was not enough and soon gardening was stopped, a victim of the National Health Service's bureaucracy that decreed central marketing of hospital supplies. The deterioration, miserable for the staff and patients, was highlighted in the *Bedfordshire Magazine* of summer 1970 in a drawing by Bernard West, whose home was in Willington but who was highly regarded throughout the county for his topographical sketches in newspapers and magazines. He bemoaned 'the lovely garden front of Moggerhanger Park dominated by the unlovely Brussels sprout in old age' – the weeds had taken over, the walled gardens and frame yards were left to dereliction (fig. 43). Nineteen seventy was a bad time in the countryside too. Bernard West noted all the good trees and hedges gone from the surrounding fields, and he concluded ominously, 'one even fears for the future of Sheerhatch itself'.

Moggerhanger Park Hospital was finally closed in 1987. In November of that year the local papers wrote of the 'doomed Park Hospital' which was 'to close and never re-open'. The thirty-eight remaining patients were to be moved into Bedford and the 'elegant' house was to be sold. It was a sad and inglorious end after sixty-five years of honourable service to the people of Bedfordshire.

fig. 43 Bernard West's drawing 'the lovely garden front dominated by the unlovely Brussels sprout in old age' from the *Bedfordshire Magazine*, Summer 1970.

RESTORATION AND NEW LIFE

In 1987 Bedfordshire County Council was under pressure to sell the parkland which had been bought from the executors of Frank Odell and used as smallholdings since the First World War. (Unfortunately, Soane's entrance lodge known as Octagon Cottage was lost in the process). The Council sold the mansion, gardens and the park to Twigden Homes. The development company was well aware of Moggerhanger's quality and history and their first task was to have gate piers designed in order to give the approach from Moggerhanger village some dignity. It was as though Humphry Repton's ghost had revived, ever keen on approaches.

Soon, however, the proposals to convert the house into executive offices and build a major new extension of open-plan offices and adjacent car parking caused rumblings in the architectural conservation lobby about Moggerhanger's fate. Concerns such as these always inspire research, and the archives of Sir John Soane's Museum at 13 Lincoln's Inn Fields – the museum guarding Soane's legacy and itself an influential voice in the conservation lobby – revealed the 'lost' house as being of far more merit than most people remembered. English Heritage raised its Statutory Listed Status from Grade II* to Grade I. (The stable block was listed Grade II.) This made it an imperative to save and restore the house with charitable grants and public monies. With the support of the Heritage Lottery Fund, the Pilgrim Trust, the Leche Trust, the Getty Grant Program and English Heritage the house and its immediate surroundings could be saved.

In 1994 the now semi-derelict Moggerhanger Park was leased by the Centre for Contemporary Ministry (known as 'Harvest Vision'), for £1. With other Christian charities they were to occupy the converted stables and use the restored house as the base for their residential teaching ministry. Summer openings to the public were allowed. The house's 'spiritual heritage' from the Thorntons and their close connections with William Wilberforce and the reforming Clapham Sect had inspired Dr Clifford Hill of the Centre for Contemporary Ministry to feel that Moggerhanger was their suitable home. In his book *The Wilberforce Connection*, published in 2004, Dr Hill portrays the eighteenth- and nineteenth-century Christian reformers, including the charismatic preacher John Berridge, the Vicar of Everton, who surrounded the abolition of the slave trade and slavery and draws the parallels that might engender equivalent reforms in society today.[67]

The ownership of Moggerhanger Park and the task of restoration were vested in the Moggerhanger House Preservation Trust established in 1997. The following year the Trust acquired Garden Wood and the walled gardens with the help of a Landfill Tax Grant, and John Phibbs of Debois Landscape Surveys was commissioned to research and report on the restoration of Repton's park and the gardens. In 1999 the London architectural partnership of Peter Inskip + Peter Jenkins was appointed to carry out the restoration, with Peter Inskip as Project Architect, responsible for gathering in all the experts in conservation building and decoration that were required.

Allied to the interpretation of Soane's drawings, the first painstaking task was the transcription of the journals, day books and accounts for the years 1790 to 1826 that had been kept in Soane's Museum since the dates of the final entries. It was intended to restore the house as Soane finished it for Stephen Thornton in 1812. Soane's meticulous accounting and naming of his craftsmen – to a standard rare among architects – allowed details of materials and decorations to be ascribed to each room, and further revealed the high standards and sophistication of the work done by the best craftsmen of their day. A forensic examination of the house's structure, the layers of paint and wallpapers, and the uncovering of the secrets of screens and cupboards, allowed Moggerhanger to tell its own story. For instance, a label was found on the back of joinery in the upstairs Night Nursery showing that it had been dispatched 'Pr Baileys Waggon' on 13 October 1810, and the account of the London joiners John and James Perry confirmed the cost of the carriage. London-sourced materials and fittings were expensive, even in the early nineteenth century, and labour was comparatively cheap. In all the changes made to the house nothing was thrown away, it was simply reused, and thus the restoration architects found themselves with something of a jigsaw puzzle to reconstruct. Most remarkably very little had been lost – the Ionic columns missing from the Eating Room were found in an outbuilding. The front door was surprisingly intact, and careful analysis revealed 'a line of what is certainly early 19th century brown paint and could well be the original scheme'.

The front door is both an end and a beginning. It 'introduces the very integrity, the 'puritan modesty' which the house has preserved unto itself through more than two hundred years, and which palpably enchants and even inspires those who enter'. The front door opens on the continuing story, which is told in the pages that follow.

NOTES
Full details of the source books appear in the bibliography.

1.   During the gestation of this book the two Repton Red Books have come to rest in the Lois Hunt Red Book Collection, Heveningham Hall, Suffolk. John Phibbs located a copy of Repton's (Beeston Leasowes) Supplement, 1798, in the British Library BL RP 5265, and Caroline Hotblack traced the 'lost' 1792 Red Book through the salerooms, and located both original volumes.

2.   Inskip, *Georgian Group Journal*, vol. xiv, 2004, p.216.

3.   John Keyworth, quoted from Soane's resignation letter, 1833, in *Sir John Soane: Architect & Surveyor to the Bank of England*, Bank of England Museum, 2004.

4.   *English Place-Name Society, place names of Bedfordshire and Huntingdonshire*, Mawer and Stenton, 1926, Godber, *History of Bedfordshire* 1984 and noted sources.

5.   Godber, p.12.

6.   Allen, A.R., *The Parish Church of St Edmund's (or St James's) Blunham*, 1993.

7.   Godber, p.378.

8.   Pym, *Sentimental Journey*, 1998.

9.   Sale particulars, 6 May 1784, Bedford & Luton archives.

10. 'shrubbery' – the term usually credited to Henrietta Luxborough (1699–1756) for her planting of lilacs, philadelphus, hollies, bays, myrtles and shrub roses in her garden in Warwickshire. See Brown, *My Darling Heriott*, 2006, pp.200ff.; also Laird, *Flowering of the English Garden*, 1999, chapter 3. Early use of the term, confined to professionals, suggests that Nathaniel Richmond (1724–84), who had worked for William Pym at The Hazells and for George Lane Parker at Woodbury Park, Everton, in the 1760s, may have been consulted on Robert Thornton's garden. (Unpublished thesis on Richmond by David Brown, Landscape Architect, Cambridge).

11. Sale particulars, 6 May 1784.

12. BL Add. MSS 45116, f.44; 38389, f.4b; 38486, f.296b (fragmentary papers) reveal his masterly signature, his brushing away of any suggestions by the 1786 Inquiry on Trade that imports of Russian linen threatened home manufactures, and his making short shrift of the misfortunes of a member of his syndicate financing the building of a sugar refinery in St Petersburg.

13. Thomas N. Thornton, *The Thornton Families of England*, 2004. Godfrey Thornton and the Sierra Leone Company, see Atkins, p.194.

14. Darley, 1999, p.18.

15. Soane's Museum is unique in that he was both acquisitive of antique examples and other architects' works and kept every paper and object of his own.

16. SM Journal no. 2, p.293. Henry Holland senior, the successful builder, friend and colleague of Lancelot 'Capability' Brown, had died in 1785, leaving control of the firm to the architect Henry Holland, who thus had three roles, as architect, builder and developer (of the Hans Place estate in Chelsea). See Stroud, *Henry Holland*, 1966.

17. Inskip, *Georgian Group Journal*, 2004, p.216.

18. See Whitbread, *Plain Mr Whitbread*, 2007, and Godfrey Thornton's place in Garrard's 'Sheepshearing at Woburn'.

19. Austen, *Mansfield Park*, 1814, ed. R. W. Chapman, 1923, 1982 edn, p.53.

20. George Byng, Viscount Torrington, was bankrupted and forced to sell Southill; it was bought by Samuel Whitbread in 1795. John Byng's hauntings of the lost country of his childhood thus had a sharpened observation as well as a poignancy.

21. Byng, Monday 19 May 1794, vol. 4, p.25; also Monday 12 May, vol. 4, p.16. Girtford Bridge was built in stone by the Turnpike Trust, 1780.

22. Byng, 21 August 1790, vol. 2, p.275.

23. Byng, 28, 29 May 1792, vol. 3, pp.10–11.

24. Repton born 21st April 1752.

25. Repton, Red Book for 'Mogenhanger', introduction August 1792. More comprehensive coverage of the Red Books will be found in John Drake's essay, pp.154-179.
26. John Phibbs, Debois Landscape Surveys, report, Moggerhanger House Preservation Trust, 2000.
27. Repton 1792 Red Book noted by Phibbs.
28. Ibid.
29. Ibid.
30. Godfrey Thornton acquired these eleven acres from Samuel Sutton in 1789.
31. Repton, Red Book 1792.
32. Greenhouse design was in its infancy, see my *Art and Architecture of English Gardens,* 1989, p.228 for William Newton's experimental construction drawings of *c.*1760. Repton became interested in them, designing elaborate glasshouses for the Brighton Pavilion and Woburn, but he does not appear to have designed a greenhouse or conservatory for Moggerhanger.
33. Repton Red Book 1792, he was obviously pleased with his previous work at Hazells Hall and Moggerhanger is demoted by comparison.
34. Phibbs, 2000 located this additional Red Book during his research, BL RP 5265.
35. Darley, pp.107–8. Haverfield had worked in the royal garden at Richmond.
36. Repton's *Memoirs,* ed. Ann Gore and George Carter, 2005, pp.137–8.
37. Soane worked for several of the Bank's directors, see Atkins, pp.182–199.
38. See Richardson and Stevens eds., *John Soane Architect, Master of Space & Light,* Royal Academy, 1999.
39. Soane's oval breakfast room SM 3/3/10v; see Darley, p.123, also Hague, *William Pitt the Younger,* pp.212–13.
40. Hannah More (1745–1833), writer and bluestocking, sympathised with Wilberforce and the Clapham evangelists. She wrote tracts for them (*Village Politics,* 1792), set up Sunday Schools and weekly classes, and became an advocate for education for girls.
41. Forster, *Marianne Thornton 1797–1887,* 1956, p.23. In this 'domestic biography' E. M. Forster explains his Thornton ancestry.
42. Darley, pp.98–99.
43. This quality of revelation comes only from a forensic examination of the structure.
44. June 1809 elevation SM 3/4/2.
45. Inskip + Jenkins Conservation Plan, 2 April 2000, p.2.
46. Wood and Dawkins, *The Ruins of Palmyra etc.,* published in 1753, see also Stuart and Revett, 1762.
47. Austen, *Northanger Abbey,* p.150.
48. Houfe, p.191.
49. SM Private correspondence (Soane and Stephen Thornton) II.T.7.6, 8.
50. Marden Hill see Watkin, pp.126–151.
51. Sale particulars 4 August 1857.
52. Elizabeth, daughter of Revd Sir William Henry Cooper Bt, was married in 1818 to George Augustus Frederick Dawkins (1791–1821). Her second marriage in 1836 to Revd Edward Henry Dawkins (1794–1859) produced one son, Edward Henry Frederick Dawkins (1837–1912). Apart from Elizabeth's own family fortune, the Dawkins also had a considerable West Indian fortune; the paintings left by Caroline Dawkins were likely to have been the legacy of James Dawkins of Clarendon, Jamaica (1722–*c.*1759), connoisseur and collector and the discoverer of the ruins of Palmyra, with Robert Wood. *The Ruins of Palmyra otherwise Tedmor in the Desart* was published in London in 1753. (Additional information kindly supplied by Jean-Pierre Brun of Moggerhanger, April 2010).
53. Godber, p.466.
54. Ensor, *England,* 1870–1914, 1936, edn 1988. p.119.
55. Ibid, p.116.
56. Additional information on Godwin College kindly supplied by Margate Local History Museum.
57. F. B. Smith, *The Retreat of Tuberculosis 1850–1950,* 1988, pp.222–3.
58. Sir Robert Philip, 'The Present Day outlook on Tuberculosis', in *Collected Papers on TB,* 1937, pp.235–6.
59. Moggerhanger Park memorandum 14 January 1920, BRO papers relating to NIV 1 (bundle in purple tapes).

60. Roy Jenkins, *Asquith,* 1967 edn, pp.262–3.
61. The Colony moved to Papworth Everard in February 1918. It took the name of Papworth Village Settlement in 1929.
62. BRO ref. CCA 155 brown manilla envelope BLARS.
63. All NIV 1 papers BRO in purple tape.
64. William Pettifer was still working at the garden in 1946.
65. BRO now Bedfordshire & Luton Archives and Records Service (BLARS). Refs. CC NIM 1–3 are the Minute Books.
66. See John Drake, *Wood and Ingram, A Huntingdonshire Nursery 1742–1950,* Huntingdon 2008, for details of the Moggerhanger etc., order.
67. Clifford Hill, *The Wilberforce Connection*, Oxford UK & Grand Rapids, Michigan 2004.

Previous page: **fig.** 1 J. M. Gandy, *Public and Private Buildings Executed by Sir John Soane between 1780 and 1815,* exhibited at the Royal Academy, 1818.

Understanding and Restoring John Soane's Work at Moggerhanger

Peter Inskip

TWO

*I*t is the contrast between the two states that Soane developed at Moggerhanger House that is so interesting. One would be exaggerating the case to say that the 1790s house, created by extension of a modest dwelling of about 1750, was an important Soane building. It has to be seen as a straightforward commission to which the architect responded in a professional manner with a very competent design. Godfrey Thornton was given a house with handsome cornices and elegant chimneypieces, but the only element that was outstanding was the lozenge-shaped dressing room on the first floor. When compared with other houses by the architect, the 1790s Moggerhanger lacked the skilful planning which was the foundation of his best designs.[1]

By 1812, that house had been crafted by the architect into a great work of art for Godfrey's son, Stephen Thornton, and it is clear that the quality of the building reflects the development of the close friendship of the architect and his clients that developed over two generations. As the relationship grew, Moggerhanger became a site of architectural experimentation and innovation. The seeds of this are visible in Godfrey Thornton's time with the proposals for a breakfast room in 1797, but it is full blown in Stephen's: the monumental telescopic chimneystacks of the kitchen pavilion, the top-lit stair hall at the core of the plan, the tribune and the pendentive-domed entrance hall all anticipate key projects that Soane was to implement years later. The house is also an important work of the Greek Revival.

Used for most of the twentieth century as a hospital, it has been rescued from near dereliction by the Moggerhanger House Preservation Trust. With so many of Soane's buildings altered or lost, the house is notable for the degree to which it survives intact. Moggerhanger is also important because it informs us about so many of his buildings that have disappeared without photographic record. It is much more representative of the architect's mature work in London than any other of his surviving buildings. In its north façade one can appreciate the style of New Bank Buildings, the National Debt Redemption Office and Praed's Bank, all of which have been demolished; the tribune tells us of the Bank of England, and something of the quality of the lost interiors at the Westminster Law Courts is apparent in the stair hall.[2]

Moggerhanger is one of the best documented of Soane's works, and the archives in the Sir John Soane's Museum allow an insight into the architect's working methods, revealing his relentless pursuit of originality and perfection. It is surprising that Moggerhanger does not appear in J. M. Gandy's composition *Public and Private Buildings Executed by Sir John Soane between 1780 and 1815* exhibited at the Royal Academy in 1818 (fig. 1). Does this imply that it was a project suppressed by the architect as he was not happy with the design for some reason? However, the drawing is as interesting for the buildings that are omitted as for those that are included. It has to be noted that none of the projects that he designed for the extended Thornton family that commissioned Moggerhanger are present, suggesting that the omission relates, not to quality, but possibly to a respect for the privacy of the passionately evangelical family.

DESIGN AND BUILDING HISTORY

The design of Moggerhanger cannot be fully appreciated without understanding how it evolved. The Thorntons were successful bankers in the City of London and were partners in the firm of Down, Thornton & Co. For several generations they were directors of the Bank of England and it was at the Bank that Godfrey Thornton met John Soane, who had been appointed its Surveyor in October 1788. It was natural, therefore, that Soane should have helped Thornton with the alteration of his newly acquired house in Bedfordshire. Soane's initial survey carried out in 1790[3] (fig. 2) records a two-storey house known as Muggerhanger Lodge with a raised plinth, string course and modillion cornice below an attic with dormers set in a plain tiled roof. Constructed in red brick, typical of the time, the elevations were limewashed a pure white. The sash windows were set in the wide exposed sash boxes still commonly used outside London, where such details were prohibited because of the danger of spread of fire. Its decidedly provincial quality, however, was lifted by a pedimented entrance door with a gothic fanlight on the south side. A small stable building was attached by a carriage house across the east end. We know that there was an earlier house on the site, but stylistic grounds suggest that the house surveyed by Soane was constructed sometime after. Its small size reflected the fact that it was only for occasional use since the family continued to live and work in London.

Muggerhanger Lodge was extended by Soane in 1791–2 with a hall and a drawing room on the ground floor below a dressing room and bedroom on the first floor (fig. 3). The enlargement produced an L-shaped plan and turned the entrance from the south to a smart, new, three-bay front facing east. To allow this reordering, the old stables were cleared away and a new block was

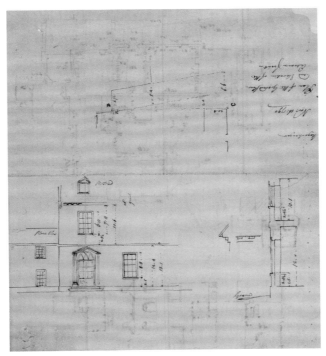

fig. 2 John Soane, Moggerhanger House survey of the elevation, 16th November 1790.

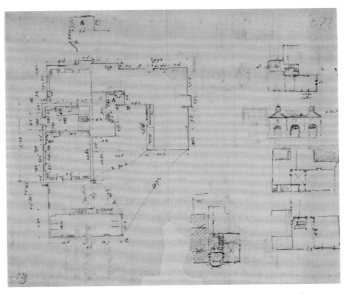

fig. 3 John Soane, Moggerhanger House survey including plan and measurements,
16th November 1790. East is at the foot of the plan.

constructed defining a stable yard to the west. The new stable building was two storeys high and five bays wide with single-bay, single-storey wings. It was designed in a round-arched style similar to his stables at Tendring of 1784. The main block contained the stabling, and the wings were carriage houses.

The entrance front, (figs. 4 and 5) illustrated in the perspective included in Humphry Repton's Red Book of 1792, had a small rectangular Ionic portico, the roof of which formed a railed balcony outside the window of the new dressing room. Repton had been introduced by Francis Pym, for whom he had prepared a Red Book for nearby Hazells Hall in 1790. His involvement in replanning the park at Moggerhanger started as soon as the house was finished with the Red Book dated 1792. However, the commentary on the *View from the Drawing Room* reveals Repton's concerns about practical aspects of Soane's planning:

> There is a difficulty in the management of this view, from the drawing-room window being placed so near to the door of the house; because it is almost impossible to preserve an air of neatness under the windows of a drawing room (especially when they are so very low) while the hall door requires an expanse of gravel for coaches to turn upon, and is exposed to the occasional defilement of Horses waiting at the door, and immediately under the windows. I am aware that this disposition of the rooms was not a matter of choice at Moggerhanger, such inconveniences being often unavoidable where Genius is confined to the altering of an old house, instead of having full latitude to plan a new one; but it is necessary for me to explain the difficulty, and point out the manner in which we may best obviate the inconveniences arising from this proximity of the drawing room and the Entrance. I propose that the road shall pass in the form of a neat gravel walk under the drawing-room window to the door, and return by a sweep at some distance behind a shrubbery . . .[4]

Repton's concerns did not result in any immediate revision to the house, but the scheme for the park was realised. A new drive from the north to serve Soane's east entrance was introduced and the old drive was removed, leaving the south side to become the garden front. Typically, Repton felt that one estate in a neighbourhood should be dominant and Moggerhanger was treated as subordinate to The Hazells, a view towards which he includes in the Red Book.

In 1798, Repton was back at the site preparing supplementary designs to his following the enclosures of the parish, which allowed for the extension of the designed landscape south beyond the immediate park. Repton introduced clumps of trees to the south and sank the road so that the view might continue well into the distance. A cottage was proposed as an eye-catcher, and a garden alcove was constructed on the perimeter of his earlier pleasure grounds to take advantage of the new prospect. However, once again, he was critical of the house, suggesting the introduction of a

figs. 4 and 5 Humphry Repton, Red Book for 'Mogenhanger', 1792, view from the east. The existing view (top) shows Soane's first re-modelling, and Repton's modifications (bottom) improve the approach and setting.

trellis verandah and a small ogee dome to dress the plain south front that Soane had largely retained from the 1750s building.[5]

The activity generated by the enclosures also appears to have been the catalyst that brought Soane back to the house in 1797. Moggerhanger, only the size of a parsonage, was clearly too small and proposals were made for doubling it by building westwards into the stable yard.[6] These, however, were followed with more modest schemes for alterations to create an oval breakfast room within the existing shell, and finally for one in a new single-storey pavilion at the west end of the south front.[7] The latter was to have had a pendentive-domed ceiling which anticipated that in both the entrance hall that Soane eventually built at Moggerhanger in 1810–12 and the architect's own breakfast room at 13 Lincoln's Inn Fields of 1812 (figs. 6 and 7). In the end, work was restricted to some redecorations, and instead of altering his house, Godfrey Thornton turned his attention to improving the lot of his tenants, possibly following the example of his neighbours at Southill and Cardington where Samuel Whitbread and John Howard had provided decent well-planned dwellings rather than decorative *cottages ornées*.[8]

Above: **fig. 6** Detail from a composite view of Lincoln's Inn Fields, showing the breakfast room looking south, 1822, by Joseph Gandy.

Right: **fig. 7** John Soane, Moggerhanger House, external and internal perspectives of extension with proposed breakfast room, 1797.

fig. 8 Moggerhanger's Gothic Lodge, built 1806, originally thatched, at the entrance from the
Bedford road, and demolished *c.*1960.

Godfrey was succeeded in 1805 by his eldest son, Stephen Thornton, and within a year,
Soane was again at the house. The resiting of the 1792 drawing-room chimneypiece to the Old
Parlour suggests that an earlier one had been retained *in situ* when the house was first enlarged, and
a new chimneypiece using Reigate stone with dove grey marble slips was carved by James Nelson as
a replacement for the drawing room. However, the main works of 1806 concentrated on the ancillary
buildings.[9] A new stable yard was formed, this time to the west of the 1792 stables. It was enclosed
by a single-storey range, divided by a dung pit, to provide more stabling and a carriage house. The
stables in the 1792 building were reversed to open off the new yard, but its wings were converted to
a brewhouse and laundry and were left to face towards the house across the old yard that now became
dedicated solely to the kitchen offices. The 'old entrance lodge' was taken down and rebuilt, with
the architect's accounts recording thatch, yew tree columns and gothic windows[10] (fig. 8).

Stephen then returned in earnest to the enlargement of the house, reviving Soane's first 1797
proposal to transform Moggerhanger into a substantial country house. Alternative schemes for
extensions across the west side were produced in 1807. Each maintained the entrance front on the
east side of the house that had been built for Stephen's father, and extended the south elevation
westwards with a breakfast room and Eating Room. The articulation of the enlarged elevation with
a central semicircular bay recalls Saxlingham (1784). The variations were primarily in the internal
planning of the hall in order to introduce a dramatic sequence of circulation spaces, one with a
Greek Doric hall which clearly relates to Soane's contemporary work at Tyringham[11] (fig. 9).

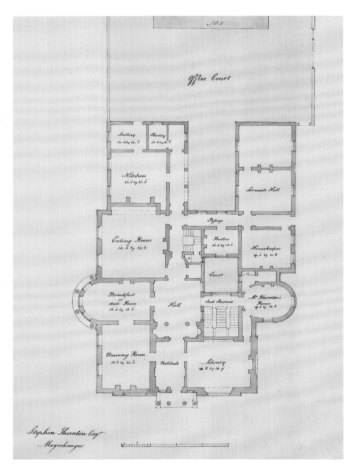

fig. 9 John Soane, Moggerhanger House, ground floor plan proposed 1807. The east front is at the foot of the picture.

In anticipation of construction, the existing house was resurveyed in 1808.[12] However, yet further variations on the plan followed, but this time based on the idea that the east entrance should be abandoned in favour of one on the north, which previously had been very much a subordinate elevation. The proposals for the reception rooms were unchanged, but the north entrance and staircase hall at the core of the building shifted the centre of gravity and provided a much more cohesive plan. This gave Moggerhanger the character of a new house rather than one subject to accretive extension. Fortunately, the distancing of the entrance from the reception rooms resolved Repton's concern of 1792. Soane prepared three schemes for discussion based on the idea of a two-storey building planned around a three-storey core. *Design No. I* was rectangular with a two-storey elevation to all sides; *Design No. II* cut back over a single-storey entrance hall to give a 'U'-shaped plan to the first floor.

Design No. III rotated the 'U' to face the garden (figs. 10 and 11). It was the second that was developed to give the present house[13] (fig. 12).

The north front was a design that was unparalleled in British domestic architecture. Its composition around a single-storey entrance pavilion was a judicious assembly of masses that produced an effect of vast size in a comparatively small house. It also provided an overture to what lay inside: the semicircular portico introducing the visitor to the square plan of the entrance hall.

The scheme also necessitated the recasting of the east elevation from an entrance front to a garden front. This was achieved by the introduction of a delicate, iron and timber, two-storey verandah in place of the stone, Ionic entrance portico of 1792, and the replacing of the two gable pediments over the side bays of Godfrey's house with one shallow pediment that unified the whole elevation.

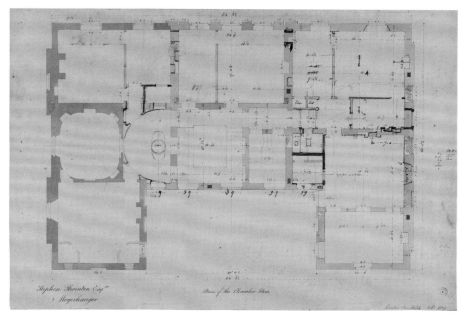

fig. 10 John Soane, Moggerhanger House, first floor plan proposed February 1809,
the curved walls of the Dressing Room, later Boudoir, remain in the centre of the east front.

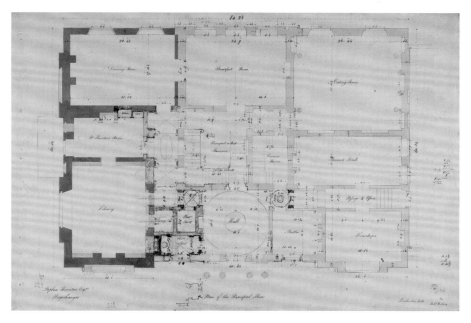

fig. 11 John Soane, Moggerhanger House, ground floor plan proposed
February 1809.

fig. 12 The north entrance front photographed in 1924.

The verandah also masked the stepping forward of the central bay on the first floor to accommodate additional space resulting from a minor remodelling of Mrs Thornton's dressing room.

On the south side, Soane's earlier idea of the central bow was abandoned in favour of a very flat elevation which breaks forward only slightly on the central three bays which are set beneath another shallow pediment, this time supported on the simplest giant unmoulded pilasters (fig. 13). The composition accommodates the closer spacing of the windows to the centre drawing room, the sashes of which rise into the wall above them to allow clear openings on to the terrace, and contrast with the greater sense of enclosure provided for the Eating Room and old drawing room that lie either side[14]. The single-storey verandah that extends across the whole of the south elevation came late in construction and appears to follow on from the completion of, and the Thornton's delight with, the new verandah on the east that had been designed as early as July 1809. It necessitated the bricking up of parts of the completed elevation to provide a flat wall at the back of the additional structure and this truncates the giant pilasters which stop uncomfortably at the verandah's roof level. However, the verandah itself is a delight and it is likely that the Thorntons would have recalled Repton's fanciful recommendation for one in 1798 in order to improve the south elevation of Soane's first house. The verandah employs the same cast-iron garland panels and timber framing with Greek key enrichments as are found on the east with the addition of '10 handsome cast iron columns 11ft

figs. 13 and 14 John Soane, Moggerhanger House, June 1809 elevations
for the south front (left) and the north front (right).

4ins long' which were supplied by Cutler and Macnaughton in December 1811 and frame each of
the principal openings. The doubling in width at the central bays corresponds with the main drawing
room within with which it is unified when the windows are open, integrating the interior of the house
with the garden beyond. The elevation of the south front dated 10 June 1809 shows none of this
and the giant pilasters on the centre bays extend down to the ground. Opening up the house for
repair has shown that the pilasters were built as the drawing, and that they were truncated and filled
in at ground floor level to accommodate the verandah.

The remodelling of the external envelope was substantial. The pitched roof of the whole of the
1791 house was removed and replaced with the present mansard construction that continued around
the complete U-shaped plan. Parapets were introduced and dummy windows provided symmetry
where openings could not be placed
because of existing chimneybreasts.
What is more, the mansard roof and
balustraded platform of the low tower
gave it a (no doubt deliberate) up-to-
date French flavour (fig. 14).

No drawings exist for the 1812
kitchen that was built as a single-storey
pavilion within the earlier stable yard
(fig. 15). However, the 1812 building
accounts include comprehensive
entries for its construction.[15] It was
possibly intended as a freestanding
block since all the schemes show the

fig. 15 Moggerhanger House, the restored kitchen wing and court.

'passage to the offices' terminating at the door to the yard, and this is confirmed by the slight lack of alignment between the pavilion and the house that is evident in the passage that connects them. However, the building that links the kitchen to the house and contains the servants' hall is clearly contemporary, but must have been conceived, like the south verandah, after construction had commenced.

Within the house, the rooms can be divided between the three periods of construction: the old drawing room at the south east corner of the house and the bedroom above it, although predominantly recast by Soane, are the only survivors of the pre-Soane building; Mr Thornton's dressing room and library to the north with Mrs Thornton's dressing room and bedroom above are from Soane's extension for Godfrey Thornton of 1791–2, and the rest of the house is from the rebuilding of 1810–12 for Stephen Thornton.

The architect's handling of the circulation through the interior is masterly. The north–south axis from the semicircular portico is developed, across the square, semidomed hall, though the double height staircase hall to the centre drawing room is cleverly juxtaposed with the turning of the axis of the house as one moves up the staircase to gain the remarkable vista eastwards across the stair well, through the circular landing, to Mrs Thornton's dressing room.

As with many of Soane's houses, the Eating Room is the grandest apartment in the house, and at Moggerhanger, it is nearly square on plan and of great originality. To achieve the clear span, Soane used composite trussed girders which resulted in downstand beams on the north and south sides of the room. The architect exploited this to give longitudinal screens supported by Ionic columns either side of the room in contrast to the conventional arrangement of transverse screens across the ends of the room; thus providing a generous extension of the corridor into the space on one side and a distancing of the landscape on the other. This disengages the core of the room which is left to focus on the dining table. The concept is reinforced by the subtle stepping of the ceiling planes (three levels within the subordinate spaces and a further three in the core) which culminate in a deep recess over the centre of the room.

The first floor was planned to celebrate Mrs Thornton's dressing room, which acted as the ladies' sitting room. It is worthy of note that a room from the 1792 extension should be retained as the culmination of the 1812 house; the only modification being the introduction of a remarkable layered window treatment that adjusts the earlier room to the new two-storey verandah outside. The lozenge-shaped treatment of the space with its ceiling divided into rectangular compartments, its walls modulated by flush pilasters supporting a frieze that is interrupted by arched recesses which recall columbaria, and the simplest white marble chimneypiece articulated by two black marble lines are Soane at his very best.

It is no surprise that Soane also paid attention to the attics which accommodated bachelors' bedrooms at the centre separating male and female servants' dormitories in the wings. To make best use of the volume, he arched his ceilings into the roofspace enclosing the roof trusses as transverse divisions articulating the rooms. The walls are inclined, answering the lower planes of the mansard roof, and producing a parabolic effect with the ceiling. The limestone chimneypieces are of remarkable quality, given their location.

Beyond the house, Stephen Thornton's stable range of 1806 on the west side of the stable yard was extended to provide further loose boxes and accommodation for the horse engine used to raise water to the head of the house. The north end of the stable yard was enclosed with the construction of a new, freestanding carriage house whose north wall was treated as a blind arcade that anticipated work at Chelsea Hospital. A glazed conservatory screened the south end of the yard from the garden.

Stephen Thornton was squire at Moggerhanger for forty-five years and died in 1850. He was succeeded by his eldest son, another Godfrey, who rebuilt the conservatory. He died in 1857 without issue. Stephen's other children were by then established in other houses of a similar social status. As Moggerhanger was not an ancient seat, there appears to have been little incentive for another member of the family to take it on. The estate was sold in 1858 to the Reverend and Mrs E. H. Dawkins. He died only a year later and his widow employed an architect named William Slater to build a church and parsonage house in the village to his memory in 1860–1. Their son stayed on at Moggerhanger until 1885 when Richard Mercer acquired the property. The two drawing rooms had been combined into one room sometime before the sale, but the Mercers appear to have been responsible for some alterations to the house in a Soanian style which included work in the best staircase and library. After the death of Richard Mercer in 1904, Moggerhanger passed to the Fanes, who converted the 1806 carriage house to further stables because of a passion for hunting. The young family of four sons resulted in the rearrangement of the nursery.[16] The house was occupied by Godwin College, from Margate, in the First World War, and the Moggerhanger estate was acquired by Bedfordshire County Council in 1919 to provide a county sanatorium and smallholdings. The use of the building as a hospital caused remarkably little change to the house since most of the wards were in new wings clad in corrugated iron that extended out into the garden from the corners of the building.[17] The landscape structure of the pleasure grounds survives, but agricultural use has resulted in the loss of many of the parkland trees.

SOANE AND THE THORNTONS

It is clear that Soane developed a close friendship with the Thorntons[18] and this is reflected in the quality that he brought to the house through his continuous refinement of the design over a period of twenty years. Not only had he worked for Godfrey Thornton in 1792 and 1797, but, as discussed, he had carried out substantial works at Moggerhanger for Stephen from 1806 until 1812. After that, for the next twenty years the architect had continued to give advice and in 1835 Stephen had sought his help in repairing the greenhouse and hothouses following a tremendous hail storm that had broken 1,900 panes of glass.[19] In addition, the installation of a new chimneypiece and other alterations were carried out under Soane's guidance in the Thorntons' houses in Grosvenor Square and Harley Street.[20]

When the Baltic trade, upon which Stephen Thornton's fortune had been based, collapsed in the 1830s Soane lent his patron £500 at 5 per cent interest to tide him over. Another client, the Duke of Buckingham, did not fare so well. In 1833 he applied to Soane for a loan of £5,000 'for the sake of an old friendship', but Soane declined. Instead, the architect offered to purchase Renaissance manuscripts and antique gemstones from Stowe for £1,735 for his own museum where they remain today.[21] Mr Thornton was clearly a less risky proposition, but what is more the family were important to Soane as sincere friends as well as clients.

In 1812, the year Moggerhanger was completed, Soane was also working for Stephen's brother William, who had assumed the name of Astell in 1807 upon inheriting his grandmother's family estate in Bedfordshire. Everton House was an early eighteenth-century gentry house, set in the village next to the church. Soane designed a conservatory that extended between its two wings and helped modernise the interior with new chimneypieces.[22] In 1818 Stephen's youngest brother, Claude, who had married the daughter of the banker, Samuel Smith of Woodhall, bought Marden Hill in Hertfordshire. Soon after he wrote to Soane: 'Having as you know purchased a residence & estate in Hertfordshire & got possession of the same, I am now able to form some idea of what I must do in the way of putting the house in a comfortable condition. But although I do not think that much need to be done, I am desirous (following the steps of my Brothers under your kind and friendly auspices) to consult you in the business... a trifling alteration to improve the dining room.' He thought that most of the work would be 'confined to painting and papering'. The works were far more extensive and the whole of the house, designed by Francis Carter as recently as 1790 was remodelled into an exquisite series of intricate Soanian spaces.[23]

Soane worked for other patrons over periods of a similar length of time to that which he worked for Godfrey and Stephen Thornton, but this usually involved different properties. For the 1st Marquess and the 1st Duke of Buckingham, this meant that he had been commissioned in sequence for a house in London, work at Stowe, alterations at Brasenose College, Oxford, proposals for Sudeley Castle and the rebuilding of Wotton Underwood. However, with Godfrey and Stephen Thornton, the work was primarily focussed on one project and this resulted in Moggerhanger being carefully reconsidered and adjusted over the years into a great work of architecture. In my opinion, the intensely personal development of the design is probably only paralleled in Soane's oeuvre in his own house at Lincoln's Inn Fields which was successively crafted and rearranged as the Museum from 1812 until his death in 1837.

Another alliance with the family was Godfrey's cousin, Samuel Thornton, a banker who with their cousin William Wilberforce was a passionate advocate of the evangelical Clapham Sect. He was also a director of the Bank of England and had inherited a fortune of £600,000. In March 1799, Soane negotiated for him the purchase of a house in St James's Square. The architect's plans for alterations do not appear to have been carried out, but over the next fifteen years he looked after the repair and renovation of the building. In addition, Soane was involved with Samuel's country house, Albury Park, Surrey, where he implemented a series of proposals in 1802. Samuel became one of the four life trustees of Soane's museum when it was established by Act of Parliament in 1833 and the architect's respect for him resulted in an engraving of Thornton being hung in the breakfast room at 13 Lincoln's Inn Fields.

CONSTRUCTION, RESTORATION AND DECORATION

The construction of Moggerhanger House reflects the changing nature of the building industry at the end of the eighteenth century. Improvements in transport meant that much of the production process was in London rather than the provinces. All of the craftsmen were Soane's favoured tradesmen who worked on many of his other houses.[24] The accounts record the manufacture in the metropolis of windows and doors, marble chimneypieces and plaster enrichments and they include for packing cases and 'carting to the Inn'. Specialist suppliers were also in London: John Flaxman RA provided plaster busts in 1796, Coade and Sealey manufactured the artificial stone balusters for the parapets at 5s. 0d. each in December 1809 and the plasterer William Rothwell supplied substantial quantities of 'Parker's cement', a patented metallic stucco based on London clays, for finishing the elevations. Materials came by sea around the East Anglian coast and down the Ouse and Ivel to Sandy where they were unloaded at Girtford Bridge, a mile from Moggerhanger. Only fifty years earlier the situation had been quite different and mid-eighteenth-century building accounts generally show everything procured locally, with only the finest crafts and materials, such as gilding and glass, supplied from London (fig. 16).

London-based construction, however, did not alter the fact that materials remained expensive at the beginning of the nineteenth century, while labour was still comparatively cheap. Their reuse is evident at Moggerhanger. Fielded and panelled doors were salvaged from the

fig. 16 Moggerhanger House, timber delivery note, 13th October 1810, found in the house during restoration.

pre-Soane house and incorporated on the second floor of the new. Redundant doors from Soane's first campaign were set aside and reused in the day nursery. The same also applied to rather more important elements: the 1792 chimneypiece in the first drawing room was relocated to the old parlour when it was redecorated in 1806; all the schemes for the new north elevation prepared in 1809 show the 1792 Ionic portico redeployed from the east front to the north (fig. 14) – the earliest surviving drawing showing the Doric, semicircular portico was not until 1810.

The use by Soane of standard details at different periods is characteristic of the architect and is best seen in the joinery. Panelled doors and shutters of 1792 are formed with a series of stepped planes, a detail also found at Chillington (1785–9) and Aynhoe (1799), while those of 1812 are treated as flush doors with the panels defined by his favourite sunk mouldings. The sunk mouldings had become favoured from 1806 onwards, the date when he had observed some rushes growing near Stowe that had suggested the idea to him as a reference extending the primitive origins of architecture.[25] In the same vein, the strigilated iron balustrade found on the generous staircase is a detail more associated with the 1790s than the second decade of the nineteenth century. Analysis of the building accounts indicates that only a fraction of the ironwork needed can have been supplied in 1812 and the balance must have been salvaged and reused from the much smaller 1792 staircase that was replaced.[26] Standard details also meant the repetition of designs. The beautiful white marble chimneypiece for Mrs Thornton's bedroom drawn in April 1792 (fig. 17) was identical to those drawn for both Mr Dillingham at Letton in 1786 and a Mr Patterson;[27] that resited to the Old Drawing Room was the same as in the governor's office at the Bank of England, and later used as the basis of the design for a memorial to the secretary of the Bank in Southwark Cathedral. Soane also recycled designs for complete rooms and a new library at No. 49 Grosvenor Square for Robert Knight designed in 1802 was a replica of Mrs Thornton's dressing room in Bedfordshire built ten years earlier.[28]

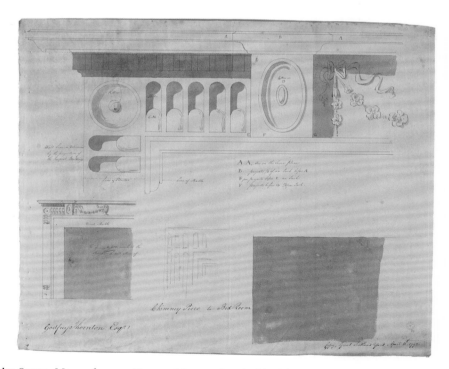

fig. 17 John Soane, Moggerhanger House, chimneypiece in Mrs Thornton's Bedroom, proposal April 1792.

Both the 1792 and 1812 campaigns involved the adaptation of an existing building and this gave rise to the use both of stucco and dummy windows. The original house was built with slightly rustic red bricks, but those of 1792 were more precise. The 1812 alterations to the house, however, were in a grey stock. This not only applied to the large extension on the west, but also to the raising of the walls to form the parapets and shallow pediments where the existing walls were brought in line with the new work. To unify his addition with the old house, Soane used stucco in 1792 and he repeated this approach when he enlarged and recast the building twenty years later. The 1812 ashlar block ruling of the elevations would have necessitated the replacement of the earlier render. Accounts record William Rothwell supplying Parker's Patent Metallic Stucco 'jointed and coloured to imitate stonework including reveals' and for 'cutting off part of old colouring from the East front of House and old stucco from South front'.[29] The Metallic Stucco was chosen because of its longevity, and the fact that much of it still survives is a credit to its inventor.

Dummy windows are present in both campaigns and are characteristic of adaptation. The east elevation was given a symmetry when it was extended in 1792 by placing dummy windows across the blind section of the wall of the original house to balance the new windows to the north. Except for the omission of the internal mouldings, each was constructed as a full-blown sash window glazed with crown glass set in front of a black painted void six inches deep. The extension and adaptation of the north front resulted in repeating the exercise in 1812, and there the spun glass was carefully selected to correspond with the arch-headed windows.

In the use of the latest services, Moggerhanger stands in advance of all its neighbours. One of the most expensive items in the 1812 accounts was the installation of a piped water service. Water closets were installed, one off the entrance hall and another on the first floor; sinks were provided in the scullery and the housekeeper's room. The prime reason for building the tower at the centre of the house must have been the housing of the water tanks to give an adequate head of water. Remnants of the horse engine supplied by William Good survive in the new engine house sited over the well in the stable yard. Soane's interest in artificial lighting is also evident with John Thwaites & Co. delivering in 1812 'a strong brass arm to carry a lamp to run upon rollers on a wheel of 18 inch diameter supported on 6 brass arms to attach to handrail of stairs'.[30]

The drawings and the extensive references to Moggerhanger in Soane's journals also tell us much about his method of working. The production of the large number of alternative schemes demonstrates how carefully the design was considered in the office. Not only are there variations on each scheme, but finished office drawings were reworked by Soane's hand with a spontaneous ink line. The drawings were sent round to Godfrey Thornton for consideration at his house in Austin Friars or at the Bank and this gave rise to further studies: three designs for the stables, delivered on 9 March 1792, were followed by three more taken round by Soane himself on 15 March.[31]

Soane's presence on site was of great importance. The actual survey notes of the existing house were made by him at Moggerhanger in November 1790, not by an assistant. During each of the campaigns, he was frequently in Bedfordshire to inspect the work as it progressed. Travelling was a major expense reimbursed by the client and the journey took all day. 'Left Moggerhanger at half past eight, walked to Biggleswade, from thence Leeds coach to London by half past ten at night. Expenses £1. 5s. 6d.'[32] The total journey was about fifty miles of which the walk was five. On other occasions, he was more fortunate. 'Left Moggerhanger at nine o'clock with Mr Stephen Thornton and his son in chaise to Town, got home by four o'clock.'[33] Such visits were sometimes coupled with inspecting other projects nearby and Soane records going from Moggerhanger on to Everton, Wimpole and Tyringham. Frequently he would stay the night with the Thorntons while Moggerhanger was still usable. On an occasion when he was going on to Tyringham, he stayed the night at the Swan in Bedford (rebuilt in 1792 by Henry Holland for the 5th Duke of Bedford). Sometimes on these visits, Soane also kept abreast of work by his contemporaries: Mr Thornton took him on horseback over to Southill in 1797 to see the great house that was being remodelled by Holland for the brewer, Samuel Whitbread II, and on a return journey in 1810 he 'called at Haileybury and saw college', just completed by William Wilkins.[34]

fig. 18 Moggerhanger House, the restored east front with verandah and a balcony to Mrs Thornton's Dressing Room above.

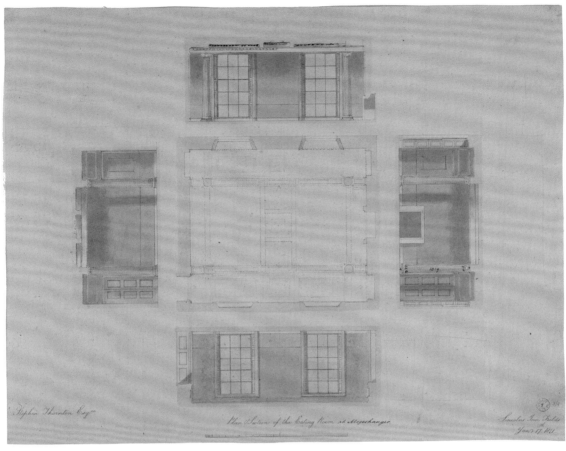

fig. 19 John Soane, Moggerhanger House, plan and internal elevations of the Eating Room, proposed January 1811.

Soane's visits to Moggerhanger meant that the house as built does not necessarily follow the final drawn scheme. Certain items were added, others simply omitted. An example of the former is the introduction of the south verandah, referred to above, which appears to have been very much instigated by a client delighted with the new east verandah (fig. 18). Other items might have been too theatrical for the evangelical Thorntons. A drawing of 1811 shows identical windows, complete with shutters, on both sides of the eating room, although those on the north would have had to be dummies and glazed with looking glass as they were at the core of the building (fig. 19).[35] By responding to the windows on the south side that look out on to the lawn, they would have given the Eating Room a remarkable symmetry and would have provided further evidence of Soane's interest in the use of mirror. The square reveals that were constructed, however, are too small to accommodate the dummy windows, and microscopic paint analysis by Catherine Hassall has demonstrated that these have never been disturbed. Sadly, it indicates that the delightful conceit was never implemented.[36]

Microscopic paint analysis was also used as an archaeological tool, and revealed that the blank openings on the ground floor between the stair hall and the best corridor that were present in 1990 were late 19th-century introductions in the style of Soane. Although Soane had indicated these on his drawings, he appears to have abandoned the idea of the blank openings during construction, realising that the design would be stronger if the arcaded treatment was reserved for the first floor of the stair compartment. Introducing a blank wall strengthened the north–south axis from the front door to the drawing room; restricting the arches to the first floor accommodated the change of axis to west – east that opened up the stair to the circular landing and Mrs Thornton's dressing room with its view on to the verandah.

Paint analysis has shown that Soane's decorative schemes at Moggerhanger gradually moved from the conventional to being decidedly architectural. The 'sporting lodge' that had been acquired by Godfrey Thornton was a white, limewashed brick building. To unify the extended house in 1792, Soane had the elevations stuccoed and limewashed a pale Bath stone colour. John Crace is recorded as 'colouring the fronts' when working at the house for Godfrey Thornton around 1797. The 1812 decoration was much more dramatic.[37] The walls were rendered with Parker's Metallic Stucco ruled

fig. 20 Moggerhanger House, the restored Entrance Hall, the oak graining originally by William Watson, 1812.

as ashlar blocks and finished with a thin coat of a similar material, acting as a kind of limewash. The 'straw-colouring' was significantly darker and richer than twenty years earlier and extended over the Ketton stone dressings and Coade stone balusters; the lattice-work verandahs on the garden elevations were also painted a similar, but not identical, colour.[38] However, while the windows had been painted a stone white to blend with the elevation in 1792, a strong contrast was introduced in 1812 with the windows painted black over a charcoal undercoat, and the front door and its frame a dark foxy brown. The later decoration thus emphasised the openings as a series of deep voids and provided considerable modelling in the elevation.

A similar coloured limewash was also applied to the grey brick kitchen wing and the red brick stables. As with the treatment of the kitchen passage, the limewash gave a unity to the buildings while the different underlying finishes of brick or render supported the hierarchy of the site. Hierarchy also applied to the proposals put forward for the decoration of the ancillary buildings. Cost would have determined that joinery on outhouses and cottages would have been brown because earth pigments were by far the cheapest. However, there is a very charming touch in Repton's 1798 suggestion that the door of the cottage that he proposes as an eye-catcher should be painted green:

fig. 21 Moggerhanger House, Mrs Thornton's Dressing Room, alterations to the window in response to the introduction of the east verandah, 1810–12.

> This cottage should be so ornamented by flowering shrubs, & by painting the door and windows green, that it may not appear the humble habitation of a poor labourer, but rather the reward of some favourite Servant, made comfortable by the elegant attention of the Ladies who may be supposed to take pleasure in decorating this little Spot.[39]

Inside the house, the treatment is also architectural in that the decorative scheme reinforces the progress of the visitor: the entrance hall is treated as a dark space with every surface grained as oak boards, including the ceiling for which Watson charged 2 guineas for 'shading ... in imitation of boards' (fig. 20).[40] The large flower at the centre of the room was painted and bronzed as were the raffle leaf ornaments on the pendentives. The hall was followed by the double-height staircase hall painted a soft dusty pink, and, finally, the lightness of the south-facing, generously fenestrated drawing rooms was complemented by violet walls. The decoration of the interior was held together by using a palette

Above: **fig. 22** Moggerhanger House, wallpaper found in
the Library, with silver flowers and green verditer border.
Right: **fig. 23** Moggerhanger House, a restored attic bedroom.

of related colours; the pink of the staircase hall responding to both the buff of the Eating Room and
the violet of the drawing rooms (fig. 21). The more private rooms were domesticated with small-scale
patterned wallpapers; that in the library with simple floral motifs in silver leaf on a stone-coloured
ground was edged with applied borders painted verditer green (fig. 22); those in the bedrooms were
of even smaller scale and matching papers were used in both a bedroom and its dressing room.

Throughout the house, silvery grey woodwork reinforced the unity: doors and architraves,
window sashes and shutters, the flush dado, were defined only by Soane's favourite sunk mouldings,
and the single and triple staff beads that outline archways were all painted the same grey. The
exception to this was where doors were grained; the oak graining in the hall extending to every
surface, and the satinwood graining in the library taking in the window sashes and shutters being
allied with verditer green architraves and dado. However, in the Eating Room, while the buff of the
walls extends over the dado and the architraves surrounding both the doors and the windows, the
sashes and shutters themselves are painted the silvery grey, and demonstrate the underlying unity
of the house. Ceilings were generally painted a greyed-white.

Soane's care in the design of Moggerhanger extended to every space, and the attics and kitchen
offices were no exception (fig. 23). It is understandable, therefore, that his approach to decoration
should have included these areas. Here the palette of the main rooms translates to sand coloured

fig. 24 Moggerhanger House, the restored staircase. The building accounts suggest that the strigilated balustrade is re-used from the 1792 house, with additional ironwork, 1810–12.

walls with the silvery grey joinery, but the actual doors themselves are painted gloss black.

The circulation spaces within the body of the house continued the dusty pink with grey detail from the best staircase including the tribune, the second stair, the circular landing and the corridors (figs. 24 and 25). However, in the kitchen pavilion the circulation spaces were whitewashed. The decoration of the passage from the hall through to the kitchen pavilion, thus reinforces Soane's characteristic subdivision of the space into a series of individual areas linked by archways. Those nearest the centre of the house are painted pink on smooth plaster, in response to the presence of Mr Thornton's business room; beyond this, pink on coarse plaster outside the butler's and housekeeper's rooms, and beyond those, whitewashed brick as the passage is by then within the single storey kitchen pavilion. Silvery grey doors occur within the pink area of the corridor, gloss black in the kitchen section, and the door dividing the two parts is painted grey on the polite side and black on the servants' side.

After the simplicity of the rest of the house, Mrs Thornton's dressing room must have come as a complete surprise. It was constructed as part of the 1792 extension and provided a ladies' sitting

fig. 25 Moggerhanger House, the restored landing, the tribune over the circular landing (top) and the perspective from the top of the stair (bottom left). The tribune in the Best Corridor, created 1810–12 (bottom right).

room on the first floor; an arrangement that the architect was to repeat at Marden Hill and at Pelwall. The room was obviously admired and its retention is apparent in all of Soane's schemes for recasting the house. In both the 1792 and the 1812 houses, the decoration of the dressing room was in marked contrast to the rest of the house. The sharp-edged polychrome scheme with its gold details and glazed finishes would have had a strong impact on the visitor as it was approached by corridors, stairs and landings which were all painted the same: probably all grey in 1790 and soft pink with grey details from 1812. Commensurate with the more conventional 1790s house, the room was painted green with the panel borders grained a straw-like colour and edged with glazed deep brown staff beads. A gilded line extended along the head of the panelling and around the arched doorway. The cloudy blue ceiling was picked out in white; some gilding and a single line of vermilion were used to highlight its different sections. The dressing room was completely redecorated in 1812 following the same general pattern as the 1792 scheme, but using different, brighter, colours and with stronger contrasts. The building accounts mention grey, pink, black, gold, 'clouded' and graining.[41] The green on the panels and upper walls was replaced with a vermilion pink. The satinwood graining was renewed and covered with a rich yellow varnish and the outlines of the panel borders and edges of shelves were done in pure ivory black and then glazed. More gilding was introduced: the rod and ribbon at the base of the cove to the ceiling was fully gilded, and additional gilding was placed around the modified window (figs. 21 and 26).

As with the construction of the house, both materials and craftsmen for the decorations were London-based. John Crace was responsible for work at the house in 1797, when his account records 'repairing and refreshing the clouded ceiling . . . and varnishing the whole of the gilding' in Mrs Thornton's dressing room, and he is likely to have been responsible for those in 1792. The decorations carried out in 1812 were executed by William Watson, the painter and glazier who worked consistently with Soane on nearly all of his later projects including the Gothic Library at Stowe and the rebuilding of Wotton Underwood after the fire of 1822. As well as the limewashing of the stucco outside and general decorations within the building, Watson's accounts identify that he was also responsible for the decorative detail: painting the 'ribbons and wreaths' (fig. 26) on the ceiling of Mrs Thornton's dressing room, the oak graining and bronzing of the Ketton stone chimneypiece and plaster enrichments in the hall, and the bronzing of the iron balustrade to the staircase. Watson was still being used at Moggerhanger as late as 1835 when he is recorded as reglazing the greenhouse and hothouses following a severe hail storm.[42]

The use of such high calibre craftsmen under Soane's direction allowed what was a very simple decorative scheme to be elevated because its execution had an emphasis on quality and precision that never faltered. Finishes were of considerable importance: outside, while the dark windows appear to have been given an almost matt finish, the front door was highly varnished; inside, each colour was cut-in with the greatest accuracy, and in the dressing room flatted paints were given a sharpness by the use of the glazes applied to the staff beads that edged them.

Soane's frequent presence on site also influenced the decorations. The blue scheme first

fig. 26 Moggerhanger House, Mrs Thornton's Dressing Room, later known as the Boudoir, the decoration painted by William Watson in 1812.

proposed for the Eating Room was replaced with a buff one with grained satinwood columns when the work was realised; (fig. 28) in several rooms paint analysis found trials below the first decoration and identified that colours were tinkered with in execution to ensure that they were just right.

Conservation policies guiding the recent restoration of Moggerhanger determined that the building should be recovered to reflect the final state of the house as developed with Soane over a period of some forty years, since he continued to advise at Moggerhanger for another twenty years after the 1812 alterations. For the decorations, this has largely meant the reconstruction of the 1812 scheme, since that state was carefully maintained by Stephen Thornton until his own death in 1850. It was not until the second half of the nineteenth century that new, more elaborate schemes were introduced with Pompeian Red decoration in the Eating Room and a great deal of gilding on the cornices. Similarly, the dark paint outside was repainted three times in the same way for Stephen Thornton before more conventional schemes were reintroduced after the house was sold.

fig. 27 Moggerhanger House, a bedroom surviving from the 1750s updated by Soane in 1792 with a new chimneypiece and joinery.

However, the restoration work has also been very much based on a conservative approach to the surviving historic fabric. Paint investigations demonstrated that Watson's original oak graining with the boards lined out in graphite survived on the east and south walls of the entrance hall, a rarity since so much graining has been replaced in other houses. This has been revealed with the removal of twentieth-century gloss paints by the conservator Sarah Warburton, who was also responsible for infilling lacunae. Similarly, removal of modern paints from the ceiling of the dressing room has recovered the decorative painting of ribbons and wreaths for which Watson was paid 3 guineas in 1812.

To restore the crispness of architectural detail that is so important to Soane's cornices, the strategy has been to remove modern paints, but leave earlier lead-based paints in place. Removal of later coats of paint has also been instrumental in the recovery of the remarkable tribune that rises up through the first floor at the centre of the best corridor. Its presence was unknown, and it was only through the stripping of the later layers of paint that the infilling of the oculus on the ground floor ceiling was revealed. It was one of the most important discoveries at the house; a favourite detail of Soane, examples of which are now rare outside the Soane Museum since so many have been lost in alterations.

The decoration of Moggerhanger is significant as it is quite different from the strong reds and vivid yellows that we associate with the architect at the Soane Museum. Its restoration has allowed the experience of the much softer approach that the architect adopted for his domestic commissions. However, while aspects are generally similar to his work at other contemporary houses such as Aynhoe, which we know from the sketches of Lady Elizabeth Cartwright made in 1834, the decoration at Moggerhanger appears to be sharper, and I would attribute that to the deep personal involvement of Soane with the Thorntons.

A Greek House

It was the publication of the first volume of *The Antiquities of Athens measured and delineated by James Stuart, F.R.S. and F.S.A., and Nicholas Revett, Painters and Architects* in 1762 that brought archaeological details of ancient Greek buildings to Great Britain. However, as Sir Howard Colvin observed 'Its effect upon contemporary English architecture has been much exaggerated; for the Greek revival was a phenomenon of the nineteenth rather than the eighteenth century, and the "Gusto Greco" of the 1760s was decorative rather than structural in character.'[43] Where it did appear with actual buildings, the Greek style was largely limited to garden monuments, and it was not until James Wyatt's Radcliffe Observatory, Oxford (1776–94) and Nicholas Revett's church at Ayot St Lawrence, Hertfordshire (1778–9) that its use for more serious building types occurs. Soane's entrance gateway at Tyringham (1789) for Godfrey Thornton's contemporary, the banker William Praed, is clearly parallel to Revett's building, and places it in the vanguard of the Greek Revival whose principal monuments were to include George Dance's Stratton Park (1803) and William Wilkins' Grange Park (1804–9), both in Hampshire.

Soane's work for Stephen Thornton transformed the 1792 Moggerhanger into a Greek Revival house. His first proposals for enlargement in 1807 included an entrance hall behind the conventional east front that he had built for Godfrey Thornton; this was based on the use of the Greek Doric order and had stuccoed walls lined in imitation of ashlar blocks. With his proposals of 1808 that moved the entrance to the north side, Soane went further and provided an exterior in the Greek form that he had used at Praed's Bank in Fleet Street in 1801 and was later to develop in the commercial buildings that he designed as part of John Nash's Regent Street in 1819. At Moggerhanger, this combined an Italian Baroque profile with the severest neo-classical details: the ground floor windows were set in shallow, pedimented projections derived from Graeco-Roman tombs, and the scrolls supporting the central tower were simplified to incised concaves. The cornice was a remarkable detail, tightly held into the wall plane, but given shadow by deep recessions between the brackets. The arch-headed windows herald the arcade that extends around the upper level of the staircase hall within.

Soane's crafting of Moggerhanger into an outstanding Greek Revival house was finally confirmed with the introduction of a semicircular portico with Doric columns. This superseded his earlier proposal for reusing the rectangular Ionic portico that had been constructed on the east front in 1792. The earliest drawings illustrating the new portico are dated 1810, and show the use of the Doric order based on that at Delos.[44] The proposals are contemporary with Soane noting on a return journey from Moggerhanger that he had 'called at Haileybury and saw college',[45] referring to the East India College of 1806 to 1809 by William Wilkins, then the most recent example of Greek revival design.

The Greek style was a completely new way of life in the first decade of the century and extended beyond architecture to furniture, clothes and even hairstyles. Unfortunately, there is no surviving record of how the house was furnished and, with the Thorntons selling Moggerhanger in 1857, the furniture has long been dispersed. However, the care taken with the refinement of the house suggests that the furnishings would also have been chosen very carefully, and one would like to imagine that Henry Moses' engraving of a contemporary conversation group with its latest Greek fashions shows the spirit of how the interior might have appeared when Soane's work for Stephen Thornton was complete in 1812.*

fig. 28 The Eating Room, as restored, with Soane's original colour scheme reinstated.

* The restoration described above was supported by the Heritage Lottery Fund, English Heritage, the Getty Grant Program, the World Monuments Fund in Britain, the Robert Wilson Challenge Fund, the Kress Foundation, the Leche Trust and the Pilgrim Trust as well as many private trusts and individuals.

NOTES

This chapter is based on an article in the *Georgian Group Journal*, Vol. xiv, 2004. It has been expanded in the light of new information following further research.

1. The Parsonage at Saxlingham of 1784 demonstrates what Soane could achieve with small houses of a scale comparable to that of his first campaign at Moggerhanger.

2. In addition the 'telescopic' chimney stacks anticipate Pellwall (1822) and Dulwich Mausoleum (1812); the top-lit arcaded stair hall at the core of the plan – the Court of the King's Bench, Westminster Law Courts (1826), and Moggerhanger's entrance hall anticipates the breakfast room at the Soane Museum (1812).

3. Survey notes etc. 16 November 1790, Sir John Soane's Museum (SM hereafter) 3/3/15.

4. Humphry Repton, *Red Book for Mogenhanger (sic) in Bedfordshire, May – August 1792* (hereafter Red Book), photographic record held at Swindon National Monuments Record Centre and at Bedfordshire and Luton Archives and Records Service (BLARS hereafter), Bedford, ref. Z/493/10–35. The Red Book, 1792 and Supplement 1798 (see note 5 below) are now located in The Lois Hunt Collection at Heveningham Hall, Suffolk.

5. *Additions to the Red Book for Moggerhanger by H. Repton*, see *Fine Books etc. from the Library of A. G. Thomas, Sotheby's 21st – 22nd June 1993'*. Repton inscribed his drawings 'To Godfrey Thornton Esq., A few pages to be added to the Red Book from his obedient and humble H. Repton', British Library RP 5265.

6. SM 3/3/10.

7. SM 3/3/17, SM Bill Book A 1797, p.353 ff.

8. The Hon. John Byng, *Torrington Diaries*, vol. 4, p.109, recorded that at Cardington, Mr Whitbread and Mr Howard 'strive which shall most benefit and adorn it, for what cannot the riches of the one and the charity of the other accomplish'. See also Gillian Darley, *Villages of Vision*, London, 1975. The cottages built by Godfrey Thornton are similar to those on the Cardington and Southill estates, see Baker pp.119–122.

9. SM Bill Book E p.217, J. Nelson, mason, February – September 1806; SM Cpbd F/16, Carpenter's account, Isaac Elger 1806. p.217.

10. Elger 1806.

11. SM Vol. 64/89 ground floor plan proposal 1807; SM Vol. 60/95 perspective from the south-east.

12. SM 3/4//34–6, 1808.

13. Design No. I SM 3/4/18, first floor proposal, November 1808; No. III SM 3/4/21.

14. SM 3/4/1 south elevation proposal June 1809.

15. SM Bill Book G and Moggerhanger Notes 3.

16. Dates on the rainwater hoppers record work done on the house in 1908.

17. Survey, plan and drawings for the conversion of the house into a sanatorium, F. W. Smart, Bedfordshire County Surveyor's Department 1919, BLARS Bedford.

18. An instance of the developing friendship is recorded in SM Journal no. 2 (1793) p.294, 'July 8th paid Newton for a workbox for Miss Thornton £3. 13s. 6d (not to be charged)'.

19. See Stephen Thornton to John Soane 10th August 1835, SM Private correspondence II.T.7.8.

20. SM Journal no. 4 (1800 and 1803) and no. 5 (1813).

21. SM Private correspondence, II.T.7.6, Stephen Thornton to John Soane, 17th December 1833; see also Arthur T. Bolton, *The Portrait of Sir John Soane*, London, 1927, p.528; Peter Thornton and Helen Dorey, *A Miscellany of Objects from Sir John Soane's Museum*, London, 1992, pp.57, 103.

22. SM 8/3/3–5 designs for a conservatory, Everton.

23. SM Private correspondence VII.B.2.3, 6 August 1818 and SM 3/2/1–5, Marden Hill 1818–19. See also Ptolemy Dean, *Sir John Soane and the Country Estate*, London, 1999, p.139.

24. Names of building tradesmen from the surviving building accounts in the Soane Museum:

1792		1810–12			
Sash frames	Mr Holland	Artificial stone	Coade and Sealy	Painter	
		Bellhanger	John Baker	and glazier	William Watson
1794–97		Bellights	Green and Pellatt	Plaisterer	William Rothwell
Painter	John Crace	Brass founder	John Thwaites & Co.		Rothwell and Cook
Cast busts	John Flaxman RA	Bricklayer	John Gray	Plumber	William Good
		Carpenter	Richard Mantell	Slater	Tyson and Sharp
1806		Carver	Robert Hume	Smith	John Mackell and Son
Carpenter	Isaac Elger	Ironfounder	Cutler and Macnaughton		
Glazier	John Hinde	Joiner	John and James Perry		
Bricklayer	J Smith and W Elson	Mason	Charles Drew		
Mason	James Nelson	Mason	Thomas Grundy		

25. SM Architecture Commonplace Book Z, 24 February 1807, f. 186; see also David Watkin, *Sir John Soane: Enlightenment Thought and the Royal Academy Lectures*, London, 1996.
26. SM Bill Book G.
27. SM 81/1/1 and 27.
28. SM 40/3/26 1802.
29. SM Bill Book G, Wm Rothwell, Plasterer's Day Account, April – May 1812.
30. SM Bill Book G, Thwaites ref. 23rd December 1812.
31. SM Journal 1, 1791, p.158; Journal 2, 1792.
32. SM Journal 5, p.83 12 November 1808.
33. SM Journal 5, p.215 3 February 1812.
34. SM Journal 3, p.212 10 June 1797; Journal 5, p.146 2 October 1810.
35. SM 3/4/9 17 January 1811.
36. Catherine Hassall, *Paint Analysis for Moggerhanger House Preservation Trust*, unpub. reports 1997–2003.
37. SM Bill Book G.
38. '304 yards Straw Colouring' in SM Moggerhanger Bill Book G, p.174, 1812.
39. H. Repton *Additions to the Red Book for Moggerhanger*, BL RP 5265, 1798, quoted in J. Phibbs, *Landscape Survey for Moggerhanger Park*, Debois Survey Group, 2000.
40. SM Bill Book G, p.239, 1812. The original graining has been revealed recently on the south and east walls, but lost elsewhere, presumably when the hall was stripped of plaster sometime in the twentieth century following an outbreak of rot, which resulted in the introduction of a concrete roof.
41. SM Bill Book G, p.240, the 'wreaths and ribbons' were charged at 3 guineas; evidence of these was revealed *in situ* in 2003, and they have been restored.
42. Stephen Thornton to John Soane, 10 August 1835, SM Private correspondence II.T.7.8.
43. Howard Colvin, *Biographical Dictionary of British Architects 1600–1840*, London, 1995, p.228.
44. SM 3/4/16, 3/4/8, 1810.
45. SM Moggerhanger Journal 5, p.146 2 October 1810.

Birchfield

Renhold

Howbury End

Grakers

Green End

6

Barford Magna

Howbury
Becher Esq.

Franklin Esq.

3

Castle Hill

4

Shelford Way

5

Remains of
an Antient Ampitheatre

Old Mill
Sluices

Castle Mills

Sluices

Willington
Mill

Ouze R.

Willington

3

5

Cople
Dog

4

5

Willington
Conduit

Cardington
Mill

3

W   I   X   A   M   T

Almonds
Farm

Sam.
Whitbread Esq.

Cople

BEEST

Howard Esq.

4

Wood
House

Whitbread Esq.

Cardington

5

LEYS

Cople
House

Long Field
Farm

6

47

3

Cople
Wood End

Deadmans
Oak

Mox Hill

High L

7

Ford
Ferry
TEMPSFORD MARSH
C A
Low Farm
PART OF
Tempsford
Tempsford
Mills
Tempsford
Turnpike
Gibralter
51
HUNTINGDON
9
Port Mahon
Foxall Wood
Ivel R.
SHIRE
Blunham
Mill
Ev
50
Ri
Asl
Meeting
Hou.
8
lunham
rlebar Esq
South
Mills
Hasell Hall
2
Fynn Esqr
Chaulton
Spur
Bridge
49
Girtford
Sandy
Cæsars
Camp
Wood
Hill
10
Girtford
Bridge
Svading
ngerhanger
Sr Philip
Monoux Bart
7
8
Fenn H
E E
R E
48
Beeston
Cross
War
Stratford
Carthag
Hatch
Beeston
Brook
End
47
Thorncote
Po
Lower Caldecot
Furzen
House
Sutton
Tur
rthill
8
9
Ivel R.
46
Short Mead
Farm
B
I

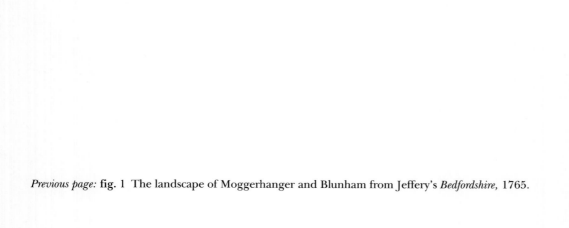

Previous page: **fig.** 1 The landscape of Moggerhanger and Blunham from Jeffery's *Bedfordshire*, 1765.

Moggerhanger in Blunham: Archaeology and Settlement from Prehistory to Parliamentary Enclosure

David Baker

THREE

*I*n 1860, Moggerhanger, Chalton and South Mills, three hamlets of Blunham, were combined as a separate ecclesiastical parish. Moggerhanger became a civil parish in 1894 and now covers 734.5 hectares (1,815 acres). The spelling and pronunciation have varied, the first found is *Mogarhangre* in the early thirteenth century. *Muggerhanger* and *Morhanger* were common alternatives. However, the preferred form today is Moggerhanger.

This essay runs from earliest prehistoric times until the enclosure of the medieval open-field system in the later 1790s, just after Soane began working for Godfrey Thornton at Park House. It is an account of what we know – some of it provisional – and an invitation to future research. It considers the landscape, its settlements and their buildings in that part of Blunham which became Moggerhanger. At least three other landscape transformations preceded the 1790s and others followed; the landscape of today contains traces from all of them, above and below ground, some awaiting discovery. As with the story of most places, there are huge gaps in the surviving evidence: no named people can be identified before the eleventh century; no surviving buildings predate the sixteenth century.

LANDSCAPE AND AGRICULTURE
BOUNDARIES, GEOLOGY AND DRAINAGE

The River Ouse provides the western and northern parish boundaries for present-day Blunham, and the River Ivel an eastern limit continuing south, until it becomes the boundary of Moggerhanger at the intersection with the former railway. This eastern boundary once ran south following a stream or drain, possibly a more easterly course of the Ivel, but recently the boundary has been altered to follow a more regular line. It is reunited again with the Ivel just north of Girtford Bridge, where it leaves the river and turns eastwards along the modern A603 road. It leaves this route at the intersection with a drain, which runs with the boundary in a curved south-easterly direction to the southernmost tip of the parish. The boundary turns northwards sharply, winding through a corner of Sheerhatch Wood and then running north-west along an irregular line that may be the result of woodland once forming Moggerhanger Park. Past Willow Hill Farm it appears to follow now removed field boundaries or the edges of present fields, crossing the Bedford road from Barford Bridge and meeting with the Ouse; it then follows the river downstream until it rejoins the Blunham boundary. The common boundary runs east–west along the line of the South Brook drain, probably the edge of the common South Field, and for much of the way also the route of the disused railway line built in the same decade as the parish was split.

Geology and relief are dominated by the rivers, with mostly low lying ground sloping towards their valleys, though a ridge of the Lower Greensand in the south-west, originally wooded, may account for the place-name, *hangra* being Old English for a sloping wood on the side of a hill. The present Sheerhatch Wood is a relic of tree cover that extended along the whole of the spur and included the site of the present park. Belts of alluvium follow the flood plains: the first and second gravel terraces are in the north of Blunham; the third terrace occupies its centre and the north-west of Moggerhanger. In the west and south-east are grey and grey-blue clays and shales, with an area of boulder clay down the centre. Several watercourses associated with the rivers, some filled and buried, may represent earlier streams before alteration for navigation and drainage, mostly on the Ivel.

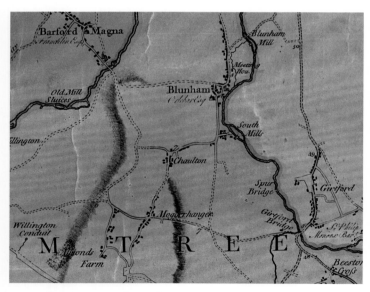

fig. 1a Extract from Thomas Jeffery's *Bedfordshire, 1765.*

A tendency to flood in Blunham made drainage play an important part in the development of the landscape, with early references to North Brook and South Brook, which survive as drains running across the parish. Manorial court rolls of 1423 record ditches as a 'nuisance'; fines were imposed in 1429 for ditches not cleaned; the rector was fined in 1433 for stopping up a common watercourse. Ponds also assisted drainage and provided a ready water supply. A field name, *Kersewell*, is recorded as early as

1240, but its location is not known. H. S. Brown's *Moggerhanger, 1777–1977* (1977) records that filling the pond behind 34 Blunham Road in Chalton took 300 carts of soil, and that an underground stream ran north-westerly across the parish to Barford Bridge.

COMMUNICATIONS

The task of tracing the changing pattern of routes and tracks in Moggerhanger starts with the earliest reasonably reliable map, published in 1765 by Thomas Jefferys (fig. 1), from which it is possible to work back and then forward in time. It shows Moggerhanger on the road between Bedford and Sandy by way of Willington and Girtford Bridge, part of the main communications framework of the pre-enclosure landscape; more localised and minor tracks and pathways are not recorded. It must be partly a creation of the medieval period and partly the incorporation of earlier routes across the landscape before the creation of parishes, along river valleys and linking strategic river crossings.

Some of these routes may have existed in Roman times, their usefulness enabling survival through the early Saxon hiatus. But a clear distinction has to be made between the straight engineered roads of the strategic military system and local roads or tracks laid out for civilian reasons, some incorporating earlier routes. It has been suggested that two Roman roads cross the parishes. The northern possibly originated at Irchester, ran to Sharnbrook, and entered the parish from Barford. Its route ran south-east across the fields to Blunham and across the Ivel at South Mills into Sandy. The evidence is doubtful at best, comprising a metalled surface glimpsed in Sandy cemetery during the 1950s, green lanes and hedgerows of uncertain origins; nothing has been seen on aerial photographs. Evidence for the other route is better though the full extent of its course is unknown; ploughed out remains west of Sandy, previously identified from cropmarks on aerial photographs and recently excavated in advance of water-main construction, comprised a sand and gravel 'agger' or raised carriageway, 8–10 metres wide, with side drainage ditches.

There must have been earlier routes in prehistoric times, but physical evidence is absent; metalled surfaces should not be expected, and the paths taken by people and their herds would have varied according to local conditions within broad corridors. Timber constructions might be expected at pinch-points involving rivers or wet ground, if they have survived in a waterlogged condition.

Moving forward a generation from Jefferys' map, the Enclosure Award of the later 1790s made some alterations to the pattern of roads as the medieval open fields were reorganised, setting out eight public roads for Blunham and Moggerhanger, with six private roads and two footpaths. What is now Park Road in Moggerhanger was created, running parallel with and south of the main west – east road; it is not a relic of a medieval 'back lane'. The route south from Blunham to South Mills used to run beside the river, but was moved further west and is now called Station Road. Several small routeways in the south of Moggerhanger did not survive. A track from Great Barford Bridge to Chalton had become a bridleway by 1836 and is now only a footpath. Jefferys shows Spur Bridge across the Ivel, midway between South Mills and Girtford, but no directly associated track. Today, surviving substantial stone abutments of an original bridge that may have belonged to the eighteenth-century improvements of the Ivel navigation support a metal footbridge.

Like many places, Moggerhanger was affected by the transport revolutions of the eighteenth and nineteenth centuries. Communication via the Ouse and Ivel must have been of local importance only until the beginning of work on the Ouse in the early seventeenth century to make it navigable on a large scale (fig. 2). The Ivel was not made navigable until 1758, with locks and sluices at Blunham Mill and South Mills and wharves at Blunham Mill for unloading and loading grain, flour and coal. New turnpike roads ran adjacent to, but not through the parish: one in use from 1772 to 1870 left the Bedford–Hitchin road near Harrowden and joined the A1 near Roxton; Jefferys shows the Great North Road turnpike running east of the Ivel. The railway came much later; the line running along the Moggerhanger–Blunham border was established by the Great Northern Railway Act passed in 1846.

fig. 2 Bradford Rudge, the Ouse Navigation near Willington, 1839.

AGRICULTURE

Both rivers have been the strongest influence on the agricultural development of the landscape. Their valleys would have been the earliest parts of the land to be cleared for primitive cultivation in Neolithic or early Bronze Age times, three to four thousand years ago. By late prehistoric times, woodland clearance may have extended over much of the area, except possibly for the southern part of Moggerhanger. Some woodland may have regenerated after the departure of the Romans only to be cleared again in early or mid-Saxon times.

Studies of aerial photographs, especially in the last twenty years, have accumulated records of extensive cropmarks for trackways and rectangular field system enclosures along the Ouse and Ivel valleys. These markings are caused by differential crop growth over the deeper soils of filled ditches, pits and postholes, easily seen on internet mapping systems such as Google Earth ™. They represent an organised later Iron Age and Roman agricultural landscape, in places overlain by later Saxon or medieval

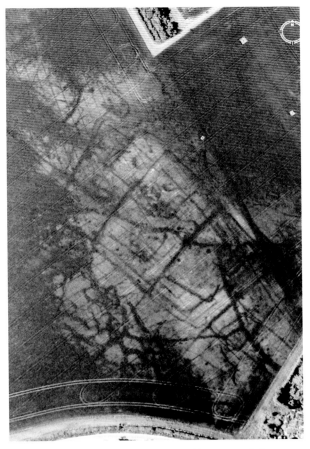

fig. 3 Fields between Willow Hill Farm and the Bedford road showing cropmarks.

open field boundaries. The most complex and visually dramatic sets of cropmarks straddle the western parish boundary around Willow Hill Farm north of Bedford Road (fig. 3) and are either side of the Ridgway; there are also well-defined rectilinear enclosures south of Park House.

The open field systems emerging by late Saxon times dominated the medieval landscape. Unfortunately no pre-enclosure map survives, but the survey of the new arrangements in 1799 does show some compact areas of pre-existing old enclosure around the centres of settlement, and extended to east and west in Moggerhanger. Using field-name evidence, a former county archivist was able to prepare an approximate reconstruction of a five open field system separate from Blunham, named as Willow Field, Clay Field, Springhill Field, Ballam Field and Beardown Field (fig. 4). Very little ridge and furrow from the medieval open fields survives as earthworks and only where it had been taken into old enclosure, or preserved as pasture or parkland. Aerial photographs

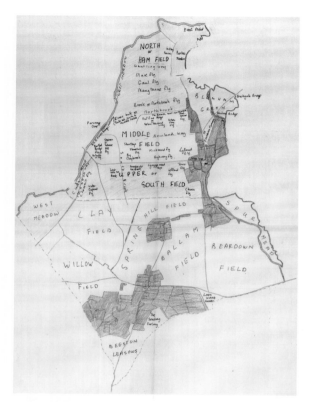

fig. 4 Schematic reconstruction of the medieval field
system between Blunham and Moggerhanger.

fig. 5 Cropmarks of medieval ridge and
furrow, south of St John's.

show fragments of the strip system as cropmarks, notably north of Willow Hill Farm and to the south
of St John's Hospice (fig. 5).

The earliest record of crops comes from the manor court rolls; in 1433 a man was fined for
trespassing with his horse and cattle on a field sown with corn, barley and peas. In the nineteenth-
century directories the crops are still recorded as wheat, barley, peas and beans, with the addition of
market gardening. The earliest record of gardeners is in the parish registers in the seventeenth and
eighteenth centuries; by the nineteenth century garden ground appears in the documents and
market gardeners are listed in the directories.

Meadowland beside the rivers and a flat open flood plain between them under constant
cultivation from at least the early medieval period would have encouraged mixed stock and arable
farming. There is also some record of the common land for grazing in Blunham, in attempts by the
Earl of Kent to regulate it in a 'charter' of 1492 when there were problems between Sandy and
Blunham; these were still being followed up in the eighteenth century when it was stated Sandy

people had no rights of common in Blunham. In 1799 the area of common meadow seems to lie beside the River Ivel; roadside verges and other waste ground were probably used for common grazing rights. Latterly there were two pounds for strayed animals in Moggerhanger in use until 1860, both of wood fencing: one was near the north-east corner of the cross-roads and opposite the Old Guinea Inn, with stocks alongside.

Sheep were a considerable element of the local agricultural economy in medieval and later times. A seventeenth-century document includes a discussion of the possibility that the Earl of Kent might not continue to keep sheep in Blunham. The parish registers record shepherds, and there was a fulling mill in Blunham in the late sixteenth and the seventeenth centuries, while weavers are also recorded at that time. Sheep were kept in some number until the nineteenth century after which there was a decline in favour of market gardening; a return of 1838 records 2,200 sheep in the parishes. The right of free warrens granted in 1315, a source of food from rabbits, cannot now be located on the ground.

Another aspect of agriculture was the harvesting and growing of reeds and osiers. The manor court roll of 1427 records a fine for reeds reaped and willows cut illegally at Glebemede. Several osier beds or holmes are mentioned in association with Mill Leases, on both the Ouse and Ivel, as are fishing rights. The double moats east of Manor Farm may have been used as fishponds.

There is a history of mineral extraction. Fifteenth-century manor court rolls record pits dug for clay as a nuisance to the whole community. Sand has also been dug on the west side of Moggerhanger, and clay pits provided the raw material for the brick kilns that functioned in Blunham in the nineteenth century. Small-scale post-medieval gravel extraction became extensive in the twentieth century in the east of Moggerhanger, beside the River Ivel.

The later eighteenth and early nineteenth centuries were the great period of 'parliamentary' enclosure, when individually owned or tenanted strips of land distributed around the open fields were consolidated into newly defined fields. This was usually a landlord-driven process but the advantages of a fair redistribution can be seen in the patchwork pattern of strips and old enclosure it reformed, exemplified in the sale particulars for Manor Farm in 1784. These described its land as 'Forty Statute Acres, three Rood, and five Perch, of inclosed Land, and One Hundred and Fifteen computed Acres, two Rood, of Open Field and Common Meadows'. Blunham obtained its Act of Parliament in 1796.

Settlement

Before Parishes

The origins of the settlements in what eventually became the parish of Moggerhanger are obscure; there is evidence for several favoured places, some of which may have moved from one to another. The area of Willow Hill Farm was occupied in later Iron Age and Roman times, distinctly west of the main medieval centres. More fieldwork is needed to tackle questions of settlement location, continuity and shift.

The presence of river gravels has helped assess prehistoric settlement. Axe implements found in Blunham gravel pits suggest Stone Age occupation in this area. Cropmarks and finds suggest late Bronze Age and Iron Age occupation along the river banks. The extent of settlement beyond the Ivel terraces is difficult to assess. There is a local tradition of two Neolithic long barrows (the 'Giants Graves') north-west of Chalton Manor Farm, about 50 – 60 metres long and one metre high, ploughed out during or just after the Second World War, but good aerial views of cropmarks in the particular field do not show any obvious evidence. The earliest known specific site is a circular cropmark near Willow Hill Farm north of the Bedford road. It represents a ploughed out 'ring-ditch' from which the earth for a burial mound was derived. A bronze armlet found in the vicinity might have been associated with a burial.

The most obvious Roman farming settlement is also in the area of Willow Hill Farm, associated with the above-mentioned Iron Age and Roman field boundaries. In 1860 workmen digging drainage ditches found Roman pottery, two quern stones for grinding corn, a burial and a coin then identified as of the Gallic usurper Magnentius (AD 350–3). Pottery from the area spans the entire Romano-British period. A metal detectorist found a fragment of a Roman bracelet in 1989, and other finds include a fourth-century coin, a bronze ring and a piece of waste bronze. Elsewhere, south-east of what later became Moggerhanger, a high status site may be denoted by finds including a small piece of mosaic floor tile, a silver denarius of Septimus Severus (AD 193–211) and a bronze radiate of Victorinus (AD 269–70). Post-Roman 'Dark Age' occupation is indicated by a find in 1934 of a pottery urn containing a sixth-century Saxon cremation, in the loop formed by Park Road, Saint John's Road and Bedford Road.

ESTATES, PARISHES AND MANORS

From middle Saxon times onwards, as kingdoms coalesced – in the eighth century this area was part of Mercia – so the effects of rising population, spreading Christianity and social stratification led to the organisation of land, the creation of estates, and the emergence of hundreds and parishes. The original parish of Blunham lies in the ancient Hundred of Wixamtree, whose meeting place may have been at Deadman's Oak on the road running out of Moggerhanger just to the south of the parish boundary.

The earliest glimpse of medieval Blunham and Moggerhanger comes from the Domesday Book compiled in 1086 by the Normans. Arranged by counties and landowners, it is concerned with property and taxation rather than topography, but something can be gleaned about settlements and agricultural resources. Blunham is mentioned in three entries and Chalton once, but not Moggerhanger. The Blunham landholders and tenants were Dominic holding one virgate from Eudo son of Hubert, the Abbot of (Bury) St Edmunds holding four hides and one virgate from the king, and half a hide from Countess Judith of Huntingdon, niece of William the Conqueror. The Chalton entry, for what later became Moggerhanger, reads:

> In 'WICHESTANESTOU' Hundred Adeliza holds CHALTON herself. It answers
> for 10 hides. Land for 10 ploughs. In lordship 5 hides; 2 ploughs there; a further
> 3 possible. 16 villagers and 9 smallholders with 5 ploughs. 2 slaves; 1 mill, 30s;
> meadow for 10 ploughs; woodland, 16 pigs. In total, value £10; when acquired
> £8; before 1066 £12. King Edward held this manor; it was Earl Tosti's. This land
> was an outlier of Potton, Countess Judith's manor, before 1066, so that no one
> could separate it from it.

Thus, Adeliza, the wife of Hugh de Grentmesnil, had a large holding of 10 hides then valued at 30 shillings. The scope for further ploughs suggests under-exploited land which may explain why the whole was still worth less (£10) than it had been (£12) when held by the Saxon Lord Tosti, who was killed fighting against his brother King Harold II at Stamford Bridge just before the battle of Hastings. The mill is presumably the original one at South Mills.

This entry, and what is known of the landscape at the time of enclosure in the 1790s, invites speculation about the pre-Conquest arrangements that gave way to the medieval manorial system. Notably, Domesday Chalton with its ten hides was more populous and larger than the other three Blunham holdings which totalled only four and a half hides and two virgates. The name Chalton itself derives from the Old English 'ceorl' (peasant or freeman) and 'tun' (farm); perhaps the place is an outlying element of a larger pre-Conquest, possibly royal, estate for which Potton, to the east, was a centre, with holdings in what became East Bedfordshire and West Cambridgeshire. The actual settlement at Chalton may be the square area of old enclosure shown on the 1799 map, respected by the medieval open field system rather than a piece carved out of it.

A similar area of old enclosure can also be seen around the present-day staggered cross-roads where the road from Chalton meets the west–east route, raising the possibility that it represents another settlement area in this outlier of the pre-Conquest estate. An alternative explanation is that it is a secondary attraction of the original centre to the main through-route where the later manorial centre established itself in the form of Manor Farm and a linear double-row development set along both sides of St John's Road. Much of the area south of this cross-roads was woodland cleared piecemeal, and some of it was later added to the old enclosure.

South-east of Manor Farm are the earthworks of a medieval moated homestead, typical of many known in this part of England. Fifty metres by sixty metres with an entrance at the south-east corner, it sits in the south-east corner of a larger moated enclosure, 80 metres east to west by 140 metres north to south, with possible entrance ways in the east and west sides. It has been badly damaged by relatively recent clearance and expansion, particularly of the internal moat, in order to provide water for the surrounding fields, but early Ordnance Survey maps and an aerial photograph taken in 1953 show authentic looking earthworks; there are cropmarks suggesting an internal rectangular structure or enclosure in the large northern part (fig. 6). The site merits closer examination, initially by field-walking ploughed ground and the use of remote sensing.

fig. 6 Oblique aerial view of moated site at Manor Farm, facing south-west.

Returning to Domesday and the mid-eleventh century, similar issues about pre-Conquest antecedents are raised by South Mills, presumably the '1 mill' in Adeliza's holding. A medieval hamlet developed there and the 1799 map shows old enclosure. Another settlement historically associated with South Mills and Chalton was the Domesday vill of *Chenmondwiche*. Historians have argued that part of its land may have been in Blunham, although the village itself was probably in Sutton. Yet that place-name (south-farm) may indicate another element of the pre-Conquest Potton-centred estate.

Going forward from Domesday, the manorial succession down the centuries, who owned or held what land from whom, is complicated, with gaps in the sequence of inheritance and transfer – fuller details can be found in the *Victoria County History*. But it seems to show the centre of significance shifting within the parish from Chalton, later Moggerhanger, in the south, to Blunham in the north. Blunham has the stone parish church with Norman work and gives the name to the parish overall.

By 1190 the Chalton holding was in the hands of the last Earl of Leicester, who granted land and a chapel to the French Abbey of St Evront. He also held the manor of South Mills or Holwells, presumably including the mill that had been part of Adeliza's holding. At his death in 1204, his two sisters gained the manors of Moggerhanger and Chalton. This overlordship passed successively to the Earls of Winchester and Derby, and the final reference in 1488 cites the Marquis of Dorset. The holding is presumably the 'capital messuage in Moggerhanger' including the 'manor and lordship of Moggerhanger' mentioned in a series of conveyancing deeds of the 1670s and 1680s, dealing with a large quantity of land in Moggerhanger, Blunham, Chalton, Thorncote and Northill. Successive transfers eventually brought the manor to the Astells, with William Thornton succeeding his uncle Richard Astell in 1777. His brother, Robert Thornton, who inherited over a thousand acres of land at Moggerhanger, sold the manor by auction in 1784 to his brother Godfrey, who eventually resided at 'Muggerhanger Lodge'.

Other medieval references to the parish are scarce but there are some pointers to the rise of the Blunham part of the parish which in 1314 was granted the right to hold a market every Wednesday, and a fair initially in July. This economic prosperity may not have outlasted the fourteenth century, as there is no further record of fair or market, except the mention of a Markyate Place in the manor court roll of 1427. In 1580, a barley badger in the parish probably traded at Biggleswade market, and later references to a water man and loader suggest waterborne trade. The cloth trade in the parish is represented at different times by weavers, fullers, a glover, tailors, a hempdresser, a silk weaver and later a lace maker in the 1850s. Other crafts and trades that took place in the parish included baking, collar making, blacksmithing, wheel turning and straw plaiting, while the parish register and directories record a midwife, cow lead, domestic servants, shoe makers, beer retailers, a rat catcher and confectionery maker living in the parish in the eighteenth and nineteenth centuries.

When South Mills was bought in 1553 by Earl de Grey of Wrest for £60, it was described as a 'fulling mill with four going stokes and two going wheels, with house newly built'. In the 1784 sale it was described as 'a water Grist-Mill, with two Wheels that work three Pair of Stones . . . [a] Lock, a dwelling-House, with various Out-Buildings, Yard and Garden, and two Closes of inclosed Meadow Land . . .'

BUILDINGS

There are about twenty-five buildings in Moggerhanger, vernacular cottages, farmhouses and farm buildings, dating from the sixteenth to the eighteenth centuries, and none earlier. No remains of earlier buildings have been excavated, though traces of post-holes and dwarf stone wall foundations from Saxon, Roman and later prehistoric times may have survived modern ploughing in places like the area around Willow Hill Farm. There is a twelfth-century reference to a chapel of unknown location in Chalton. A reference of 1802 to a former religious house on the site of a farmhouse belonging to Lady Lucas and the discovery of shallow-buried human skulls and bones, presumably nearby, is unlikely to be related, because Lady Lucas' land at enclosure seems to have been largely in what is now Blunham. Until Moggerhanger had its own church, built in 1859–61 by Mrs Dawkins of 'Morhanger' Park House in remembrance of her husband, vicars had on occasion taken services in the cottages, or villagers had walked to Blunham, where the south porch was dedicated for their use.

Historic buildings can tell us not only about themselves as structures but also about the past organisation of the places where they stand. The local historian has to contend with the lack of documentary references to often humble buildings, our ignorance about those built and demolished in the past, and the extent to which the historic character of the survivors has been obscured by alterations and extensions. The distribution of the larger farmhouses is not necessarily a good guide to landholdings and tenancies. Some may be associated with old (pre-eighteenth century) enclosure adjacent to settlements, but the distribution of holdings in the open fields prevented the compact farms we expect today. Some may have not housed farmers but farm labourers, or changed their function over the years, with larger buildings coming to house several families.

fig. 7 Chalton Farmhouse.

fig. 8 Willow Hill cottages.

The highest status buildings in Moggerhanger were the predecessor of the Park House and the Georgian Chalton Farmhouse. Assuming a reasonable degree of accuracy in Jefferys' map of 1765, and noting that it predates the insertion of Park Road at enclosure, his annotation of 'Almonds Farm' refers to the pre-Soane 'sporting lodge' rather than to Park Farm further north. The list description for Chalton Farmhouse (fig. 7) indicates later 18th century origins; there are parts of an earlier-looking building attached to this fine red-brick Georgian house, but little more is known about it.

The farmhouses all show signs of development in more than one phase of construction. Manor Farmhouse in St John's Road, of seventeenth century origins, was altered at least in the nineteenth century and shows a complicated sequence, as does Village Farmhouse further south in the same road, dated to the seventeenth and eighteenth centuries. Willow Hill cottages (fig. 8) at Willow Hill farm are described as the former farmhouse and of seventeenth century origins, but must have been considerably reworked into their present form as a pair of cottages. Bridge Farmhouse on the east of the parish is given sixteenth century origins; its 'L' plan suggests two phases and the original would have been no larger than cottages elsewhere in the parish. All these buildings are timber-framed and plastered, and the steep pitch of the roofs on those now tiled suggests they were originally thatched.

There are few surviving historic farm buildings. An eighteenth-century dovecot more or less contemporary with Chalton Farmhouse but lacking its nesting boxes and a granary with a raised

fig. 9 Barns at Willow Hill Farm.

floor at Manor Farm are both in red brick. Four early eighteenth-century barns survive at Willow Hill Farm, in weather-boarded timber frame with pantiled roofs (fig. 9). They are part of the homestead described in 1928 as comprising a brick and tile stable and stall; a timber and corrugated iron two bay cart lodge and garage; a timber and tile range comprising a five bay implement shed, a five bay shelter facing the farmyard and a six bay shelter facing the yard; two barns; seven loose boxes; a stable for eight horses; a harness room and chaff box; two calf boxes; five pigsties; a barn and a four bay cart lodge.

fig. 10 Nos. 57–69 Bedford Road.

Several timber-framed and mostly thatched cottages date from the seventeenth and eighteenth centuries. Now individual houses, they would usually have accommodated more than one family. As a general rule, those with doorways opposite the side of central chimney stacks serving two rooms are earlier than those with chimney stacks in or against the end walls. The Thorntons at the Park House were to restore several, leaving plaques to record their work, as at 57 and 59 Bedford Road (GT 1800) (fig. 10), Willow Hill Cottages (formerly GT 1791) 5 St John's Road (CCT 1813).

The essay is based by permission upon a longer unpublished and fully referenced account of Blunham and Moggerhanger, researched and written in 1979 by Alison Allden as part of the Bedfordshire Parish Survey programme. It can be found in the Historic Environment Record (HER) now maintained by the Central Bedfordshire Council, and the collections of the Bedfordshire and Luton Archives and Records Service (BLARS), both of which she consulted. The illuminating suggestions about the development of settlement in late Saxon and early medieval times were kindly provided by Christopher Taylor. Updated HER and BLARS material is at:

http://www.bedfordshire.gov.uk/CommunityAndLiving/ArchivesAndRecordOffice/CommunityArchive s/Mogerhanger/MogerhangerIndexOfPages.aspx

Previous page: The bridge and entrance lodge at Tyringham by J. M. Gandy.

MOGGERHANGER IN ITS STYLISTIC AND GEOGRAPHICAL CONTEXT: SOANE'S LATER COUNTRY HOUSES AND NETWORK OF PATRONAGE

DAVID WATKIN

FOUR

Soane is well known for his numerous country houses in Norfolk and Suffolk in East Anglian white brick, notably Letton, Saxlingham, Tendring, Shotesham, Blundeston, Ryston and Gunthorpe, all dating from the 1780s before he developed his mature personal style. It may come as a surprise that he also went on to build a large number from the 1790s onwards in Bedfordshire, Buckinghamshire, Cambridgeshire, Hertfordshire and Huntingdonshire. This essay will set Moggerhanger in the context of this group of houses, both stylistically and in terms of the complicated but highly fruitful network of patronage which made them possible (figs. 1 and 2).

It was on Soane's all important stay in Italy as a young man in 1778–80 with his Royal Academy bursary that he established his career by meeting key figures who were early patrons and played important roles in promoting his career.[1] These included Philip Yorke (fig. 3) (1757–1834), 3rd Earl of Hardwicke from 1790, for whom Soane worked at Hamels, Hertfordshire, and Wimpole, Cambridgeshire, and Thomas Pitt (1737–93) (fig. 4), 1st Baron Camelford from 1784, an amateur architect of some distinction who introduced Soane to important future patrons.

Thomas Pitt owed his peerage to the influence of his cousin, William Pitt the younger (1759–1806), prime minister from 1783–1801 and 1804–6.[2] Though Thomas Pitt employed Soane as an architect,[3] he was more important for bringing his architectural skills to the attention of William Pitt to whom Soane was to be in great part indebted for his appointment as architect to the Bank of England in 1788. It was through the Bank that Soane met several important clients, notably Godfrey Thornton, a director of the Bank, for whom he carried out the first phase of work

fig. 1 John Soane, 1795, the architect, whose work at Moggerhanger should be seen in the context of his mature, personal style.

fig. 2 Saxlingham Rectory, Norfolk, one of Soane's earlier East Anglian works of the 1780s.

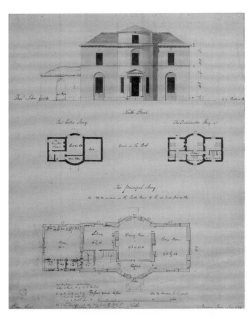

fig. 3 Philip Yorke, 3rd Earl of Hardwicke, who Soane met on his Grand Tour and for whom he worked at Wimpole Hall near Cambridge.

fig. 4 Thomas Pitt, 1st Baron Camelford, an amateur architect who introduced Soane to important clients, not least his cousin William Pitt who influenced Soane's appointment as surveyor to the Bank of England.

at Moggerhanger in 1791–2.[4] As we shall see, he also worked for other members of the Thornton family in Bedfordshire and Hertfordshire.

Thomas Pitt, Lord Camelford, a near relative of Richard Grenville, Earl Temple, undoubtedly introduced Soane to Grenville's son, George Nugent-Temple-Grenville, Earl Temple from 1779 and 1st Marquess of Buckingham from 1784. He was the owner of two great estates in Buckinghamshire, Stowe and Wotton Underwood, houses where Soane carried out considerable work for him.[5] The banker William Praed, for whom Soane was to build Tyringham, Buckinghamshire, had political ambitions which brought him close to the Marquess of Buckingham who took Soane to see Praed at Tyringham in August 1792.

HAMELS, HERTFORDSHIRE, 1783

The first commission given to Soane by Philip Yorke was for a rustic dairy (fig. 5) at his Hertfordshire estate, Hamels, near Buntingford.[6] It was intended for his future wife, Lady Elizabeth Lindsay, whom he married in 1782, and was ready for her as a kind of first wedding anniversary present in 1783.

fig. 5 Soane's design, for Philip Yorke, for a thatched dairy at Hamels with pillars of 'elm trunks'.

A perspective view of it, probably made for Soane by John Webber, shows a building with a thatched roof and a Doric portico with coupled columns at each end below a triglyph frieze and a pediment adorned with a medallion of a cow in the tympanum. On an elevational drawing of the building with two plans, inscribed by Soane 'Plans of two designs for a Dairy in the primitive manner of building', he explained the rustic character of this fully functional dairy: 'The Pillars are proposed to be the Trunks of Elm Trees with the bark on & Honey suckles & Woodbines planted at their feet, forming festoons etc. The Roof to be thatched & the ends of the Rafters to appear.'[7]

It is a realisation of the imagined primitive hut which Marc-Antoine Laugier claimed as the origin of Doric architecture in his *Essai sur l'architecture* (1753). Twice translated into English in the 1750s (fig. 6), this influential book, of which Soane owned ten copies, was his bible, while his master at the Royal Academy, Sir William Chambers, published reconstructions of primitive huts in the first plate of his *Treatise on Civil Architecture* (1759). The concept had its origins in the Rousseauesque notion of the noble savage and in *Julie, ou la nouvelle Héloïse* by Rousseau whose *Confessions* was among Soane's favourite reading. He gave Lady Elizabeth Yorke a copy of another key text in the development of confessional literature, Goethe's *The Sorrows of Young Werther*, which he owned himself.[8]

The dairy at Hamels was evidently important for Soane at the start of his career for he exhibited a design for it at the Royal Academy in 1783 and also published it in his *Plans, Elevations and Sections of Buildings* (1788), plates 43 and 45. Nonetheless, it was virtually identical to the dairy he designed but did not build for Lady Craven in 1781 at her *hameau* in Fulham.[9] The interconnection as designers between Soane and George Dance, in whose office he had spent formative years in 1768–72, was such that he called on Dance in January

fig. 6 Laugier's primitive hut in the English translation of his *Essay on Architecture* (1755).

fig. 7 Dance's dairy of *c.*1788 for Camden Place in Kent.

1783 to discuss the proposed dairy at Hamels. Dance in turned designed a dairy in *c.*1788 at Camden Place, Kent (fig. 7), which was a close echo of that at Hamels.[10]

WIMPOLE HALL, CAMBRIDGESHIRE, 1791–5

Within a few weeks of succeeding his uncle as Earl of Hardwicke in May 1790, and thereby inheriting the great house and estate of Wimpole, Philip Yorke was discussing altering the house with Soane.[11] They subsequently worked together to create what has been described as a 'coherent vision' of which 'the underlying theme is that of recapturing the past, with clear references to the golden age and classical antiquity in neo-classical dress'.[12] The foundations on which this vision was formed were laid in Italy when Yorke wrote in 1779, 'The three temples at Paestum of the old Doric order are magnificent buildings and I was astonished to find how perfect they are. An ingenious architect by the name of Soane now studying at Rome accompanied us thither and measured the buildings.'[13]

The mid-seventeenth-century house at Wimpole, greatly expanded by James Gibbs in 1719–21 for the collector, Lord Harley, had been bought in the early 1740s by Philip Yorke, 1st Earl of Hardwicke, who commissioned Henry Flitcroft to refront and alter it. Within this complicated building which must have seemed old-fashioned by the 1790s, Soane contrived the Yellow Drawing Room, one of the most stunning of his many fine interiors. To insert a room rising the full height of the existing house, it was necessary to cut away attic rooms as well as a service staircase and water closets. Soane was able to draw on his recent experience at Chillington Hall, Staffordshire (1785–9), of inserting a top-lit saloon into medieval walls. This skill he further developed at his Law Courts (1822–5) (fig. 8), where he created astonishing top-lit spaces between the buttresses of the medieval Westminster Hall.

fig. 8 Soane perfected his dramatic top-lit interiors in his designs for the Law Courts.

fig. 9 The Yellow Drawing Room at Wimpole Hall, one of the finest of
Soane's interiors, designed in 1791–1792 for Philip Yorke 3rd Earl of Hardwicke.

fig. 10 The Book Room at Wimpole, by Soane, adjoining the original
Large Library designed by James Gibbs.

The Yellow Drawing Room at Wimpole – T-shaped with a dome over the head of the T and its short ends terminating in apses – resembles a Roman Catholic chapel with a chimneypiece in the place of an altar. It is, indeed, supposedly inspired by Alessandro Galilei's domed Corsini Chapel of 1732–3 at S. Giovanni in Laterano, Rome, which Yorke had admired in 1778, commissioning a watercolour drawing of it from Soane. In fact, the space Soane created at Wimpole is probably closer to the neo-antique loggia of Raphael's Villa Madama, Rome (c.1516).

Since the Yellow Drawing Room faces north, it was necessary to provide as much light as possible, hence Soane's scalloped dome over the darkest part and his enlargement of the two existing windows on the north side. He also filled the space between these windows with a large mirror, along the bottom of which he ran a gilt balustrade continuing the stone balustrade outside, creating the illusion that the wall was open to the park. The panelled overdoors of the room, which was intended for county balls, concerts and theatrical entertainments, were provided with classical scenes in grisaille of music, poetry and drama, and its walls were hung with tart yellow silk framed in dark arabesque borders (fig. 9).

The large library by James Gibbs needed expansion to accommodate the books and state papers which Philip Yorke had inherited in 1790 from the 2nd Earl. Thus Soane cleverly extended the small ante-room of Gibbs' library two bays westward into the existing orangery where he created the Book Room (fig. 10). This has a sequence of segmental arches unusually decorated with large paterae, flat round ornaments, by the plasterer, John Papworth, featuring acanthus and lotus leaves. Soane adopted the same pattern of arch and paterae in the dining hall he created at this time within a medieval shell at Gonville and Caius College, Cambridge, using the same craftsmen as at Wimpole.[14] However, in a notable spatial development at Caius College he replaced the solid paterae with open oculi. The taut elegance of the Book Room at Wimpole is continued in the inventive design of the chimneypiece at the east end with its strips of black marble, bordered by tiny gold balls.

West of the Yellow Drawing Room Soane created a new staircase to replace the one he had destroyed and another simpler stair leading to a plunge pool (fig. 11) on the east side of the

fig. 11 The plunge pool at Wimpole, designed on an antique model with paired curving staircases.

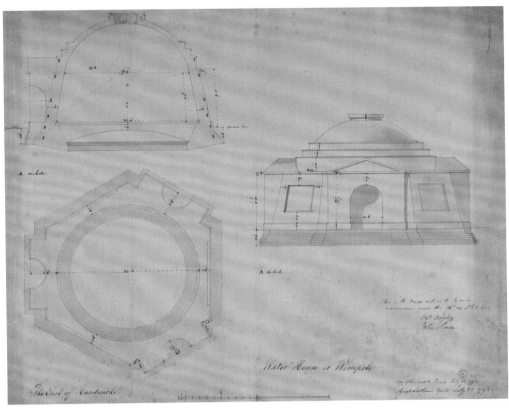

fig. 12 Soane's designs for the Castello d'Acqua at Wimpole Hall, a substantial conduit
house built in 1793, but since demolished.

second internal courtyard. With its barrel-vaulted ceiling into which is let a semicircular roof light, the pool is approached through twin staircases and a pair of tall narrow arches with balancing twin doors, an astonishing achievement on such a small scale. Soane had been impressed by the neo-antique bath complex he had seen at the Villa Albani, Rome, built by the collector, Cardinal Albani.

To provide water for the bath at Wimpole, a substantial conduit house, called by Soane a *Castello d'acqua* (fig. 12), was built from his designs in the park in 1793.[15] The fanciful title came from a competition in 1780 for a building of that name at the Academy at Parma, which Soane entered while in Italy. The neo-antique theme of the competition was inspired by the tower-like fountain buildings in Rome which terminate the aqueducts bringing water to the city. Soane's ambitious structure at Wimpole was twenty feet in diameter and surmounted by a stepped Pantheon dome, fifteen feet high. 'Its exterior representation', he frankly explained, 'is that of a mausoleum'. This curious work has been demolished but Soane illustrated it in his *Sketches in Architecture ... Cottages, Villas and Other Useful Buildings with Characteristic Scenery* (1793), and had a wooden model of it made in 1793 which survives.

As an enthusiast for agricultural improvements, the Earl of Hardwicke commissioned Soane to design the Home Farm in 1794 on a large scale round a symmetrical courtyard. The great timber-framed threshing barn is clad with weatherboard below thatched roofs in a version of Cambridgeshire vernacular. Soane also designed stables, cattle sheds, cart sheds, and even hen houses, as well as cottages of *pisé*, rammed earth or mud, echoing the Rousseauesque ideals of simplicity which he had already deployed at Hamels.

SULBY HALL, NORTHAMPTONSHIRE, 1792

Soane enlarged Sulby Hall, or Lodge, for René Payne in 1792 but it was demolished in 1949 except for the stables.[16]

TYRINGHAM HALL, BUCKINGHAMSHIRE (1793–*c.*1800)

Soane met the banker William Praed through the Bank of England and was also personally recommended to him by the Marquess of Buckingham. Praed's wife Elizabeth inherited Tyringham, an old manor house which they initially intended to remodel before deciding to replace it in 1793. The result was one of Soane's masterpieces (fig. 13), it was completely remodelled in *c.*1903–7 by Ernst von Ihne in a German Baroque manner so that little remains of Soane's interiors.[17] Fortunately the superb entrance lodge and bridge have survived. The segmental archway on unmoulded piers is marked with incised lines or bands, classical mouldings reduced to their abstract essence. These continue into the flanking, one-storeyed wings where the windows in the centre are flanked by pairs of baseless, unfluted Greek Doric columns in antis, pure cylinders of the gravest simplicity.

The whole composition is close to the abstract neo-classicism of Friedrich Gilly in Berlin, notably his Monument to Frederick the Great of 1797 which includes a monumental gateway extremely close to that at Tyringham. Soane would not have known Gilly's designs, but he learned of the work of Claude-Nicolas Ledoux who had influenced Gilly. Soane bought and annotated Ledoux's great book, *L'architecture considérée sous le rapport de l'art, des moeurs, et de la législation*, in 1804, the year of its publication. The geometrical severity of the gateway at Tyringham is echoed in the sleek form of the bridge beyond it, a single segmental arch in limestone of which Ptolemy Dean has eloquently written: 'A linear quality is conveyed by the banding across the smooth ashlar, as streamlined as the flow of the water beneath.'[18]

The bridge (fig. 14) commands a fine view at an oblique angle to the house, which

fig. 14 The dramtic bridge at Tyringham was designed to command an oblique view of the house, and illustrates Soane's scenographic skill, that is also reflected within his interiors.

Above: **fig. 13** Tyringham Hall: the largest country house which Soane designed *de novo*. It was commissioned by the banker William Praed who he met through his work at the Bank of England.

Left: **fig. 15** The dark, vaulted Doric entrance hall at Tyringham began the journey of surprise and release through the interior.

comes as a surprise because, in the manner of the landscape designer Humphry Repton, it cannot be seen from the lodge. The journey through surprise and release was continued in the house where one began in a dark, vaulted entrance hall, with Greek Doric columns in the corners as in his hall at Bentley Priory, Middlesex (1789–94).[19] Like the columns of the semicircular Greek Doric entrance portico at Moggerhanger, those at Tyringham and Bentley Priory have fluting which terminates about two-thirds of the way down the shaft. This device, known as stopped flutes, was adopted in antiquity to prevent the damage which the wheels of passing carriages would otherwise cause to the delicate fluting of columns. It was, of course, less appropriate for Soane to introduce columns of this form in *interiors*, as at Tyringham and Bentley.

The Doric entrance hall at Tyringham (fig. 15) contrasted with the central tribune, a double-height, top-lit space around which all the principal interiors were organised.[20] Brightly illuminated and with coloured glass, it provided a rich glow at the heart of the house, yet such poetry did not prevent Soane from providing up-to-date services including steam-driven central heating as well as billiard room and nurseries. The romance was brilliantly conveyed in the superb watercolours of exteriors and interiors painted for Soane by Gandy in 1798, showing the exteriors at different times of day to emphasise the shifting light effects.[21] Gandy and Soane here revealed themselves as true children of the Picturesque aesthetic.

Soane worked on larger houses than Tyringham, but these were all remodellings of existing houses. Tyringham was the largest of the eighteen he built *de novo,* and also the most expensive, at over £43,000. It also gave him his only opportunity to design the whole traditional assembly of house, offices, stables, lodges and parkland. The only feature he failed to achieve was the stunning 'Sepulchral Church' which he designed in 1799–1800 on an eccentric triangular plan, probably influenced by Laugier. Boasting a Greek Doric entrance portico and a giant scalloped dome in the interior which had three rounded apses for the altar and private pews, this would have been effectively a Praed family chapel.[22]

AYNHOE PARK, NORTHAMPTONSHIRE, 1799–1804

Aynhoe is not far from Tyringham so it was probably William Praed who introduced Soane to William Ralph Cartwright, an MP and Tory squire who inherited the house at the age of one in 1772.[23] It was a fortified manor house in origin, rebuilt in the 1660s and again in 1707 when the Baroque architect, Thomas Archer, moved the main entrance from the south side to the north where he added low, free-standing wings on each side of the forecourt. These contained stables on the east side and kitchens and offices on the west. He also doubled the length of the south garden front to twenty-five bays, creating a library at the west end and an orangery at the east.

Soane's first thought was to replace Archer's wings on the north front but in the end he added a triumphal arch to link the house to the east wing where it serves as a screen over the private road running to the church. He reflected its form with a blocked-up arch on the front of the housekeeper's room on the balancing west side of the forecourt. The triumphal arch motif echoed the theme of the entrance front of his own house, Pitzhanger Manor, and the Lothbury Arch at the Bank of England, on the design of both of which he was working at this time.

Most of his remaining work at Aynhoe was to create interiors behind existing façades, a skill he had already deployed masterfully at Chillington, Wimpole and Bentley Priory. At Aynhoe, he was able to remodel the ground floor along the south front so that six rooms open into each other through double doors in an axial vista, which was quite an achievement within the envelope of an existing house. Moreover, Soane transformed all these interiors by creating alcoves and vestibules with much interplay of curves, involving new ceilings and groin vaults, all featuring his own incised ornament and string courses with ball mouldings. His beautiful library features segmental arches of plaster, recalling those in the Book Room at Wimpole Hall.

A remarkable painting by Gandy of Soane's ante-room (fig. 16) between the library and dining room (fig. 17) shows it with Ionic columns and a dome with

fig. 16 The ante room between dining room and drawing room at Aynhoe in Northamptonshire.

ribbed umbrella vaulting, but these were omitted in execution on the grounds of expense. Soane's original estimate for the work at Aynhoe came to nearly £14,000 but in the end Cartwright was prepared to spend only just under £8,000, which accounts for some of the austerity of detail. Nonetheless, Soane was able to add a storey over the library wing so that he could create an enfilade along the whole first floor, like that on the ground floor. This takes the form of a passage punctuated by round-headed arches, from which is approached the principal bedroom which he remodelled with a dramatic screen of two pairs of coupled Ionic columns.

From 1954 the house was owned by the Mutual Householders Association who adapted it to form twenty flats, but in 2004 it was bought by its present owner who with great taste has brought it back to single owner occupation.[24]

fig. 17 The dining room at Aynhoe, 23 January 1835. This watercolour, by Lili Cartwright, illustrates how simple the detailing was in execution.

MICKLEFIELD HALL, HERTFORDSHIRE, 1800

Soane created a cross-vaulted entrance hall and top-lit staircase at Micklefield Hall for Elisha Biscoe in 1800.[25] He owed this modest commission to his friend, John Robins, auctioneer and estate agent, who supplied furniture to him for several buildings, including the Bank of England.

RAMSEY ABBEY, HUNTINGDONSHIRE, 1804–7

When Soane was designing his gem-like Gothic Library at Stowe in 1805–7, he was also at work on making alterations at Ramsey Abbey, Huntingdonshire, for William Henry Fellowes, nephew of his Norfolk patron, Robert Fellowes. William wanted the new work to be in a Gothic character to suit the existing monastic buildings, notably the thirteenth-century Lady Chapel. Soane found a modest, largely Tudor house with later additions which he made E-shaped by adding on the north front a new entrance porch with an oval vestibule opening into a striking arched corridor or 'cloister', running along the whole front. He also added a three-storeyed wing on the west side of the house containing a top-lit staircase which was replaced in a remodelling of 1838–9 for Edward Fellowes by

Edward Blore who also transformed Soane's main staircase and south front. However, he retained Soane's north front with its unusually narrow lancet windows, while enlivening its skyline with a pierced openwork balustrade which replaced Soane's parapet.[26]

STOWE HOUSE, BUCKINGHAMSHIRE, 1805–7

The Marquess of Buckingham acquired two collections of precious manuscripts, early English, called 'Saxon', in 1803, and Irish in 1804. He decided to house these in a special chamber of their own in the basement of the south front at Stowe, rather than in the two-storeyed library above.[27] The final form of the south front as built in 1772–7 had been designed by Soane's friend and patron, Thomas Pitt, Lord Camelford, for his cousin, Richard Grenville, 2nd Earl Temple. It must have been Pitt who introduced Soane to the new owner of Stowe, George Grenville, 1st Marquess of Buckingham (1753–1813), nephew of Earl Temple. For the Marquess, Soane created Buckingham House, Pall Mall, in 1792–5, a major commission in which he worked in perfect harmony with his patron.

fig. 18 The Gothic Library at Stowe House, designed by Soane for the Marquess of Buckingham, c.1805.

Deciding that the new library (fig. 18) should have an appropriate Gothic character, Lord Buckingham recommended Soane to consult the leading antiquarian, John Carter, who published a brief article in the *Gentleman's Magazine* in 1803 on 'Westminster Abbey and Henry VII's Tomb'. Buckingham wanted Soane, normally a most reluctant Gothicist, to take the brass screen of 1505–c.12 surrounding the tomb as his model for the green and bronzed book cases in the new library. Indeed, he wrote to Soane in 1806 that he had 'departed a little too much from that model', but Soane was impressed by his patron's architectural knowledge, praising him in his ninth lecture at the Royal Academy in 1815 as someone 'whose taste and skill in designing can only be equalled by the other distinguished talents and superior intellectual attainment which that noble encourager of the fine arts so pre-eminently possessed.'[28]

Soane provided a polished brass chimneypiece for the library as well as ebonised mahogany furniture inlaid with ivory quatrefoils. He also created a groin-vaulted entrance lobby with a top-lit staircase leading up to the two-storeyed library above. This demonstrates his genius in creating poetry out of small spaces, for above its groined vault the staircase is lit from a tapering hexagonal cone. This feature recalls the form of the lantern light in his Dressing Room at 13, Lincoln's Inn Fields of 1812, which he later elaborated on a large scale in his Freemasons' Hall (1828–30). At basement level on the north entrance front at Stowe, Soane created a new entrance hall in 1803, known as the Egyptian Hall because of its extraordinary canted walls and tomb-like character.

EVERTON HOUSE, BEDFORDSHIRE, 1812

In 1812, the year in which Moggerhanger was completed, Soane was working at Everton House for Stephen Thornton's younger brother William, modernising the interiors and adding a substantial conservatory with coloured glass, linking two wings; all now demolished.

MARDEN HILL, HERTFORDSHIRE, 1818–20

In 1818 Stephen's youngest brother, Claude George Thornton, bought Marden Hill which Soane remodelled for him in 1818–20.[29] The house had been built for Robert Mackay in 1790–4 from designs by the architect Francis Carter as a white brick box with a curved bay on the south front. In this it resembled Soane's early houses in Norfolk and Suffolk in the style he had evolved from architects like Thomas Leverton and Robert Mylne. After buying the house and estate at Marden Hill, Claude Thornton invited Soane in August 1818 to make what he expected to be the most modest improvements to put it 'in a comfortable condition'. He little realised how Soane would remodel it to create a ceremonial route through the centre with his customary vaulted spaces.

Soane enhanced the existing east entrance front of Marden Hill with a portico of four Ionic columns on the ground floor supporting a balustraded balcony and a first floor with a large tripartite window. This provided an accent like that he provided with his Doric portico at Moggerhanger, while it was economical to create because the columns were ones which Soane had ordered for new buildings for the Bank of England but were in the end never used. Soane improved the existing entrance hall by creating angled corners and Corinthian columns, and relocating the doors into the rooms on either side to the centre of each wall. This created a symmetrical, axial vista through the house terminating with the chimneypiece in the dining room on the north side and with the window in the reception room on the south side. The existing staircase was wrapped round the sides of the space but Soane replaced it with an elegant one in which a central single flight returned in further flights on each side. It was lit from above with a skylight in the form of a simple oval dome.

The new route created by Soane up and through the house culminated on the first floor, as at Moggerhanger, in the boudoir with its starfish vault which he formed out of a plain, existing bedroom. This magical space opens into another space at right angles to it, a vaulted lobby forming the first floor of Soane's new porch. This has a shallow saucer dome like a canopy, flanked by shallow segmental vaults, the contrast of light and shade as we move from one space to the other in the boudoir making this sequence one of the most memorable in his work. As Pevsner explains, 'The composition is so original as to be almost perverse, but the effect, although complex, is not at all confusing.'[30] It is a miniature masterpiece comparable to Soane's Dining Room at 10 Downing Street, and the Privy Council Chamber further down the street. This large window which lights Soane's lobby underlines the axial relation of the house to its setting, for it is aligned on to the long beech avenue which, unusually for the 1790s, leads directly to the entrance front.

The Marden estate adjoins that of Panshanger, seat of Earl Cowper who bought Marden in 1903 from their heirs of Claude George Thornton. Panshanger was demolished in 1953–4 and Repton's park was subsequently gravely damaged. Marden Hill is well maintained though adapted as flats.

WOTTON UNDERWOOD HOUSE, BUCKINGHAMSHIRE, 1821–2

Soane's connection with the Grenville family led to an even more ambitious commission than that he had received at Stowe. This was to rebuild Wotton House for Richard Grenville, 2nd Marquess of Buckingham, created 1st Duke of Buckingham and Chandos in 1822, the son of Soane's patron at Stowe, the 1st Marquess of Buckingham.[31] Wotton Underwood, fourteen miles from Stowe, had been since 1749 the second house on the Buckinghamshire estates of the Grevilles. When it was gutted by fire in 1820, it was a tribute to Soane's well-deserved reputation for efficiency that he was immediately called in to deal with the problem. In rebuilding the damaged house, he kept largely to the façades as built in 1704–14, though reducing the height somewhat. However, he transformed the interior by converting the simple entrance hall (fig. 19) into a great tribune, rising through two storeys surmounted by a circular dome with a glazed lantern. This anticipated the top-lit stair hall at the heart of Moggerhanger.

In early unexecuted designs for the tribune at Wotton made in December 1820, Soane showed the first floor surrounded by a ring of Ionic columns, as in his Pitt Memorial at the National Debt Redemption Office of 1818. In another of these designs, dated 13 December 1820,[32] the ground floor sports Greek Doric columns like those in the entrance halls at Tyringham and Bentley Priory. As executed, all columns on both floors at Wotton were omitted in favour of the creation of a more diaphanous space in which the first floor is supported on a bracketed gallery. This faintly echoes the hanging canopy below the ceiling in the library at Soane's house at 13, Lincoln's Inn Fields, of 1812.

Ptolemy Dean describes how in the staircase at Wotton, 'Whole areas of wall were hollowed out to give views into and through the adjacent tribune. The masonry walls are bent and curved like paper. The experience of depth and height is akin to that of a gothic cathedral.'[33] This effect was largely lost in the 1920s when many of the openings were filled in, but it is hoped that Soane's tribune will in due course be restored. The creation of a north – south corridor with arched openings, linking all three staircases, was both convenient and visually dramatic, recalling the similar effects at Aynhoe.

fig. 19 The main stair looking towards the former tribune, originally the upper part
of the hall at Wotton Underwood House (floored over in the 1920s).

It may come as a surprise that, when the Duke of Buckingham ran into grave financial problems from the late 1820s, he should have asked the modestly born Soane for the huge loan of £5,000 in 1833, 'for the sake of an old friendship'. Soane declined, but instead bought from the duke four illuminated manuscripts and 275 antique gems which he had lately acquired for the Gothic Library at Stowe. In 1833 Soane made a loan to Stephen Thornton of Moggerhanger who had been affected by the collapse of Baltic trade.[34]

CONCLUSION

It can be claimed that the group of houses considered in this essay, Wimpole, Tyringham, Aynhoe, Moggerhanger, Marden Hill and Wotton Underwood, contain the finest interiors in any of Soane's country houses, probably only equalled at Port Eliot, Chillington, Bentley Priory and Pitzhanger Manor. Moreover, the north entrance front at Moggerhanger has a Baroque character which is unique in Soane's work. Forming an aesthetic as well as a geographical group, these magical houses in a wide circle round Moggerhanger showed Soane's growing ability to transform a building behind earlier façades. Not much attention may currently be given to this skill in schools of architecture, but it was deployed brilliantly by Adam at Syon, Schinkel at Schloss Charlottenhof, Nash at Brighton Pavilion, and John Simpson at the Queen's Gallery at Buckingham Palace.

The houses we have seen were made possible not only by Soane's architectural genius but by his professional reliability, the speed and efficiency with which he carried out work with a small office, and the punctilious way in which he made frequent site visits himself, even in appalling weather, rather than leave the task to subordinates. His clients had total confidence in him, successive generations of the same family turning to him for help over long periods of time. He seems not to have shown them the prickly side of his personality, neurotic, and quick to take offence. Despite this difficult temperament, which led to disastrous relations with his sons and his grandson, Frederick, his fellow architects respected his professional probity so greatly that they invited him to accept the presidency of the (Royal) Institute of British Architects on its foundation in 1834.

NOTES

1. For details of Soane's travels in Italy, see John Ingamells, *A Dictionary of British and Irish Travellers in Italy: 1701–1800* (New Haven and London: Yale University Press, 1997), pp.876–7.

2. See Howard Colvin, *A Biographical Dictionary of British Architects 1600–1840*, 4th edn (New Haven and London: Yale University Press, 2008), pp.806–8; and Michael McCarthy, 'Thomas Pitt, Piranesi and John Soane: English Architects in Italy in the 1770s', *Apollo*, cxxxiv, December 1991, pp.380–6.

3. On his first meeting with Soane in Rome, see Ingamells, *Dictionary*, p.274.

4. Peter Inskip, 'Moggerhanger', *Georgian Group Journal*, xiv, 2004, pp.214–42.

5. See Peter Inskip, 'Soane and the Grenvilles', *Apollo*, April 2004, pp.17–24.

6. Pierre de la Ruffinière du Prey, 'John Soane, Philip Yorke, and Their Quest for Primitive Architecture', *National Trust Studies*, 1979, pp.28–38.

7. *Catalogue of Architectural Drawings in the Victoria and Albert Museum*: Pierre de la Ruffinière du Prey, *Sir John Soane* (London: V & A, 1985), pp.46–7.

8. David Watkin, *Sir John Soane: Enlightenment Thought and the Royal Academy Lectures* (Cambridge University Press, 1996), p.116.

9. Pierre de la Ruffinière du Prey, *John Soane: The Making of an Architect* (University of Chicago Press, 1982), pp.245–8.

10. Jill Lever, *Catalogues of the Drawings of George Dance the Younger (1741–1825) and of George Dance the Elder (1695–1768)* (London: Sir John Soane's Museum, 2003), p.299.

11. On Wimpole, see *Country Life*, 21–8 May 1927; and Ptolemy Dean, *Sir John Soane and the Country Estate* (Aldershot: Ashgate, 1999), pp.64–77.

12. Eric Parry, 'Wimpole Hall, Cambridgeshire', *Architects' Journal*, 26 March 1986, p.50.

13. BM Add MS. 35378 f.305v, cited in David Souden, *Wimpole Hall, Cambridgeshire* (London: National Trust, 1991), p.29.

14. On this forgotten interior by Soane, see Richard John and David Watkin, *John Simpson: The Queen's Gallery, Buckingham Palace, and Other Works* (London: Papadakis), 2002, pp.61–8.

15. See David Adshead, 'John Soane's Designs for a Castello d'acqua at Wimpole, Cambs', *Apollo*, April 2003, pp.15–21.

16. See Colvin *Biographical Dictionary*, pp.636 and 968; Royal Commission on Historical Monuments, *Country Houses of Northamptonshire*, 1966, pp.315–16; and Dean, *Sir John Soane*, p.185.

17. See Nikolaus Pevsner and Elizabeth Williamson, *The Buildings of England, Buckinghamshire* (New Haven and London: Yale University Press, 1994), pp.703–6; and *Country Life*, 1929.

18. Dean, *Sir John Soane*, p.185.

19. *Ibid.*, pp.54–63.

20. See Gillian Darley, *John Soane: An Accidental Romantic* (New Haven and London: Yale University Press, 1999), pp.107–10.

21. For illustrations of some of these, see Margaret Richardson and MaryAnne Stevens, eds., *John Soane Architect, Master of Space and Light*, exhibition catalogue (London: Royal Academy of Arts, 1999), pp.135–9.

22. See Darley, *John Soane*, p.112; and Giles Waterfield, ed., *Soane and Death*, exhibition catalogue (Dulwich Picture Gallery, 1996), p.115.

23. Dean, *Sir John Soane*, pp.78–89; and *Country Life*, 2, 9, 16 July 1953.

24. For an account of this welcome transformation, see Marcus Binney, 'Aynhoe Park, Northamptonshire, the Home of Mr James Perkins', *Country Life*, 16 July 2008, pp.81–4.

25. Peter Guillery, 'Norwood Hall and Micklefield Hall: Works by Sir John Soane', *Architectural History*, 1987, pp.181–9.

26. For illustrations of this little known work, now a school, see Dorothy Stroud, *The Architecture of Sir John Soane* (London: Studio, 1961), p. 139; and *Sir John Soane, Architect* (London: Faber and Faber, 1984), plate 157.

27. See Michael McCarthy, 'Soane's "Saxon" Room at Stowe', *Journal of the Society of Architectural Historians*, xliv, no. 2, May 1985, pp.129–46.

28. Watkin, *Sir John Soane*, p.619.

29. On this house, see *Country Life*, 22 August 1941; and Dean, *Sir John Soane*, pp.138–49.

30. Nikolaus Pevsner and Bridget Cherry, *The Buildings of England, Hertfordshire* (Harmondsworth: Penguin Books, 1977), p.246.
31. See *Saving Wotton: The Remarkable Story of a Soane Country House,* exhibition catalogue (London: Sir John Soane's Museum, 2004); *Country Life,* 1, 7, 15 July 1949; and Dean, *Sir John Soane,* pp.150–61.
32. William Palin, 'Soane at Wotton', in *Saving Wotton,* pp.28–36. fig. 21.
33. Dean, *Sir John Soane,* p.156.
34. Inskip, *Moggerhanger,* p.216.

Above: A detail from Gandy's compilation of all the works designed by Soane between 1780 and 1815, showing the architect sitting before his ingenious plans and designs.
Next page: Joseph Gandy's compilation of Views of the Bank of England exhibited at the Royal Academy in 1822.

New Bank. Buildings. in Princes Street.

North Front of the Bank, as originally Designed.

Humphry Repton, Moggerhanger and the Bedfordshire Landscape

John Drake

FIVE

A well spent country life should consist in farming, gardening, fishing, riding and in reading old and new authors – what more is man to be wish'd for? For all the rest is scandal, folly, madness! Even the littleness of country sports exceed, surely the wicked idleness of London occupations!

John Byng 1794

Humphry Repton, it might be said, cultivated being a countryman, and then turned it into his profession (fig. 1). He was born in Bury St Edmunds in 1752, spent two years at Norwich Grammar School, then aged twelve, he was sent to Rotterdam to equip himself for an apprenticeship in the textile trade. Textiles – 'the nature of calimancoes, Mecklenburghs, worsted satins' – did not interest him, but he found the Dutch gardens and music, drawing and painting suited his tastes and talents. He married at twenty-one and was to father sixteen children, though there were many sad infant deaths. He failed in business, and with a modest legacy from his parents, moved his family into the Norfolk countryside at Sustead, not far from Aylsham. There, with a little patronage from the Windhams of Felbrigg, some dabbling in politics and some income from selling his drawings, he tried to be a gentleman farmer, but when the money ran out was forced to move his family to a cottage on a busy road at Hare Street in Essex (fig. 2). Under duress, and after reading some Gothic romance, 'with almost the vague uncertainty of a dream' the possibilities of his new profession came

fig. 1 Humphry Repton 1752–1818, a likeness taken in his lifetime, and from his *Memoir*.
He cultivated being a countryman and it became his profession.

fig. 2 Hare Street, near Romford, Essex, the view from Repton's cottage; left, the *before* view, open to prying
eyes and offending smells, and right, with the flap turned back, the garden extended, screened and planted
for pleasurable occupations. An example of his professional skills.

to him. He studied techniques, acquired a ledger and some sketch books, and announced himself, in the summer of 1788 as a 'Landscape Gardener', a term of his own invention.

Repton was both well organised – sending out circular letters and having a trade card printed (fig. 3) – and he was also amiable and, on the surface, confident in his approaches. His first commission came from Jeremiah Ives at Catton in Norfolk, in 1788, and though for a start he concentrated upon his beloved East Anglia, soon he was moving further afield.

Fortunately for us, John Byng (1743–1813) was travelling at the same time. Byng, later the 5th Viscount Torrington, had been brought up at Southill in Bedfordshire, but the estate had been lost through his brother's bankruptcy. It was with nostalgia that Byng, lately a lieutenant-colonel in the Foot Guards, made excursions into the county between 1781 and 1794, often to show his young son the landscape he loved and keeping his diary.

In August 1790 he travelled through Bedfordshire, and on 21 August he comments on the sorry state of what was going to be a bad harvest:

> A month might formerly serve the harvest: now half the seed returns to earth
> e're it can be gathered, or the wet retards it, till it is half rotted – this is the
> miserable, destructive economy of the day!! – one man dying under fatigue,
> reaping away in a field of twenty acres – several farmers trust wholly to the arrival
> of Irish itinerants and know that neither the dropsy of London nor the men of
> factories constitute the sound honest laborious flesh of the nation.

By Wednesday, 1 September, we find him: 'Passing the demolished Gamlingay Park* and Everton village, I came to the Hasells, a pleasant, dry, shaded seat of Mr Pym, which is soon to be put under taste by Mr R[epton] and where Mr P has employed (already) a large sum of money in building a new house.' His diary continues on Thursday, 2 September:

> Over Gifford bridge [then through Sandy] and thence to the Hasells Mr P[yms]:–
> there is a cottage at the foot of the Warren in a lane, at the edge of his grounds,
> whose situation is truly picturesque, and retired; my wonder always was that such
> a place was not taken within his pale and improved into something more:– every
> such place of mine should hold a happy dependant to rear my poultry etc. Old
> Mr P. has as little taste about these things . . .'

* Gamlingay Park was laid out in 1712 by Sir George Downing, the founder of Downing College, Cambridge. It was abandoned in 1776 as a result of extortionate demands for lawyers' fees for an annulment of his arranged marriage, made when he was fifteen years' old.

fig. 3 Repton's famous Trade Card, his innovatory business asset, demonstrating the surveyor's art, and also an illustration of his formidable business discipline.

Francis Pym was the owner of the Hazells estate (fig. 4), south of the village of Everton, which was situated on the edge of the greensand ridge which runs diagonally across Bedfordshire. Beneath this ridge were his arable fields stretching to Sandy. Mr Pym had already employed Nathaniel Richmond (to whom Lancelot Brown handed over smaller commissions) to lay out a formal grass terrace overlooking the town of Sandy.

James Wood's plant nursery in Huntingdon records several fruit trees that were supplied to be planted in Pym's walled gardens. Pym must have announced to the local gentry in 1790 that he had chosen Mr Repton to advise on his park. Repton must have been busy at the time as he did not visit until the following year. Other fine properties were also built by rich landowners along this ridge which afforded fine views across the wide Great Ouse river valley.

Francis Pym later became High Sheriff of the county in 1791 and chairman of the Quarter Sessions, obviously choosing local politics rather than parliamentary affairs. He was an original subscriber to the Bedfordshire Agricultural Society and was present at its first meeting on 22 July 1801, becoming president in 1808. He sponsored a prize of two sovereigns for the best pen of six

South Down ewes, and a premium to the Bedfordshire labourer in husbandry 'who shall have been for the greatest number of years without interruption a member of an enrolled Benefit Society'.

Repton was a prodigious landscape gardener, in the wake of Lancelot 'Capability' Brown, whose profession gave him easy access into the upper classes in England from aristocrats to new wealthy merchants, bankers and professionals. Each of his clients was given not only landscape advice, but a wider opportunity of enriching their cultural aspirations in a society which had become much involved in the world of art.

His landscaping career came to fruition in 1788 when he was thirty-six years old and lasted for the next thirty years during which he carried out more than 400 commissions, while other pretentious landscapers were experiencing commercial failure. During this period the country was involved in the parliamentary enclosure of commons, advances in agriculture and road improvements while London experienced a large increase in population, becoming a world metropolis.

Repton established a presentation Red Book in which his proposals were explained and illustrated to every client. In it he described, as if in conversation with his client walking around the grounds, his plans, how to improve a dull scene, perhaps a new view and how to achieve it – which could be either major or minor – perhaps the removal of a single fence or a few trees. Sometimes in the final paragraph a suggestion which necessitated his returning at a later date is included.

Repton was met by Mr Pym at The Hazells when he visited the park in March, August and November 1791. Promptly in December 1791 suggestions for the improvement of the park came with the arrival of The Hazells Hall Red Book (fig. 4). Mr Pym must have been most impressed by

fig. 4 Repton's Hazells Hall Red Book, 1791, a plain watercolour illustration of the view towards Moggerhanger, the view to be opened and framed from Nathaniel Richmond's terrace walk.

Repton's suggestions as he had already started on some of them before receiving the Red Book. Repton's relationship with his client prospered and they soon became friends, culminating in a successful solution for the landscape. The Pym family's close connections to the Astells and the Thorntons were probably Repton's original introduction to Moggerhanger.

In Repton's introduction to the Hazells Hall Red Book, he referred to his discussions with Mr Pym on the Art of Landscape Gardening:

> Sir
> In the few following pages you will find little more than what I have at different times had the honour to suggest to you in conversation and indeed many of the ideas will be carried into execution before I can avail myself of the winter's leisure to deliver on paper this general plan for the proposed improvements. Yet as you have desired me thus to give my opinion in writing I will endeavour in my usual manner to elucidate some general principles of the Art I possess, an Art, which I am very ambitious of rescuing from the commonly received opinion, that it is more under the dominion of Caprice of fashion than any of the polite or imitative arts: while on the contrary I hope it may one day be proved, and perhaps these loose limits which I thus scatter in detatched volume may in some measure contribute towards proving, the true taste of the Art of Landscape Gardening, as well as in all others, may be founded on reason and fair argument.
> I have the honour to be Sir
> Your much obliged and
> Obedient humble Servant
> H Repton

Repton's subtle way of advising his client is illustrated in the following Observation in the Red Book:

> I beg leave to call the attention as elucidating a general principle in Landscape Gardening viz: betwixt the hall door and the spot from where the house is seen, a trifling swell in the ground prevents the eye from seeing the whole line of road, consequently it seems to be an awkward direction and the ground being lost beyond the ridge the road appears in contact with the house in a part where it ought not to do so; it also leads us to err in judging of the distance at which we view the house, and consequently gives a false idea of its real size, inducing us to suppose the whole building to be smaller than it really is, because we measure its size by the scale of the road while its perspective diminution is not apparent, and therefore apt not to be remembered.

Concluding his proposals Repton wrote 'This map 1791, made by Mr A Watford who took the actual survey, I have merely availed myself of it to mark by different Colours – the improvements mentioned in this book. H Repton.'

He acknowledged that a Mr Wilkins did the drawings in the Red Book. Both Wilkins and Watford were contracted to help produce the Red Book within one month of Repton's final visit to The Hazells.

Meanwhile John Byng had been out and about in 1792 visiting his home county once again. On Monday, 28 May 1792, he is staying at the Sun Inn in Biggleswade. He records his somewhat sarcastic impressions of meeting Mr Repton:

> A brilliant tho' windy morning. It should seem that I had much to do from seven (my hour of rising) till nine o'clock, my hour for breakfast. At 10 o'clock I intended to my ride but Mr Repton – the now noted landscape gardener – came in and delayed me for ½ hour: he is a gentleman I have long known and of so many words that he is not easily shaken off; he asserts so much, and assumes so much, as to make me irritable, for he is one (of the many) who is never wrong; and therefore why debate with him?
>
> I wondered that he should not keep his own post chaise and he wondered at my riding; so wonders never cease! I left him at breakfast.
>
> At 9 o'clock Mr R[epton] return'd from his visitation in this neighbourhood, to draw his plan, and to relate his journies, his consequence, and his correspondence. Scarcely any man who acquires a hasty fortune, but comes vain, and consequential; tho' Mr R – now being sought for, has a professional right to dictate, and control, and being Nature's physician, to tap, bleed and scarify her.
>
> But he is very wrong (in my opinion) in not being well mounted; and in not building a comfortable travelling chaise with good case for a Madeira wine. But to all this R is a stranger; and *piques* himself upon sleeping in fresh sheets every night (!) which hereafter he will dolefully repent.
>
> Having much discourse (for R – is an everlasting talker) we did not part till midnight'.

The next morning he recorded: 'Tuesday 29th May: A most blustering morn; and if the wind subsides, the rain will fall, for the clouds seem full. I rose at 7 o'clock; R – was up at 8, and then went off to Mr T's [Thornton] in this neighbourhood, where he is to plan and oversee. Thence I pursued my way thro' Potton, in two miles more to Gamlingay, a village in Cambridgeshire and so by Waresley Park (one of the parks to be improved by Mr R).'

Two days later: Thursday 31st May: I hurry'd to bed early last night, one of the miseries of being alone. My bed was good, and my own sheets were dry. I shall see Mr R[epton] laid up by rheumatism, wondering at the cause.'

Nº IV.

fig. 5 Repton, the Red Book for 'Mogenhanger'
1792, views from the house northwards, showing the
offending drive which brought the coach and horses
to stand beneath the windows, and the rather dull
avenue existing.

fig. 6 The flap lifted to reveal the drive passing between the two imposing elms and sweeping around into a shrubbery, where the horses can wait; the avenue has been thinned to well-spaced trees suitable for the park.

Godfrey Thornton (1737–1805) had acquired the Moggerhanger estate of 1,024 acres in 1784. Situated on a rise in the landscape between the Great Ouse and Ivel rivers to the west of Sandy the estate was surrounded by ridge and furrow farming plots and to the south is the extensive Sheerhatch Wood. Godfrey later rented the wood known as 'Garden Wood' which had grown up over some of the ridge and furrow landscape and began his own improvements including a new walled garden in 1790. A member of a nouveau riche merchant and banking family he had moved quickly up the social ladder and was a director of the Bank of England, and in 1789 as a member of the building committee met John Soane, who had been appointed architect for the rebuilding of the Bank.

Godfrey Thornton was in urgent need of a country estate compatible with his position in society, where he could entertain his friends at weekends. In 1790 he commissioned Soane to advise on improvements to his house at Moggerhanger. Godfrey's importance grew the following year when he was appointed deputy-governor to the Bank of England. The following year Soane's alterations to the house were commenced.

In 1791 the 'park' landscape around Moggerhanger would have seemed unpromising, consisting of open fields to the north of the house, a couple of mature trees, a small avenue running part of the way to Park Farm, a couple of small ponds and a small area of grazing, some paddocks and some woodland.

In 1792 Godfrey Thornton commissioned Humphry Repton to advise on the landscape. Obviously Godfrey had been impressed with the improvements he had seen at Mr Pym's estate at Everton. Repton presented his Moggerhanger Red Book in August 1792, shortly after his first visit on 28 May. His response sets out to place both the owner and the site in the appropriate social hierarchy of the time. In his introduction he states:

> Sir,
> The following pages will I hope sufficiently explain my opinion with respect to the improvement of Moggerhanger park, and also will give me an opportunity, of assigning some reasons for that opinion as I proceed. I have always considered it the duty of my profession to suggest no improvement, without some fair reason for adopting it, and everyday's experience convinces me, that altho' Landscape Gardening is often considered as more subject of fashion or caprice than any other Art, it is not less reducible to rules than Architecture or Painting since true Taste in all the Arts must be found on reason and reflection.
> I have the honour to be, Sir
> Your most obedient humble Servant
> H Repton

Obviously Godfrey was too busy in London to meet Repton when he visited the estate, compared with Mr Pym who took time to walk and converse with Repton when he visited The

Hazells. Repton skips over his idea of the *Art of Landscape Gardening*, possibly thinking Godfrey will not be impressed if he goes into the subject in some detail. He immediately gets down to the task of explaining the Character and Situation of the estate:

> The proper management of the Grounds [suggests that Repton had come to the view that Godfrey had little knowledge of running a country estate] so much depending on the Character and Situation of the house to which they belong, I confess there appeared to me some difficulty in the treatment of Moggerhanger. A park of such extent inclosed by a pale and annexed to such a command of property, requires a house of superior stile to that which has lately been repaired. It is not easy to affix its true Character, it is too small and too humble for a country-seat, and at a distance from the capital is too great to permit its being called a villa.
>
> I shall therefore consider it as an occasional sporting-seat; and as I do not see any situation in the park greatly preferable to the present for a larger house, I must suggest such improvements as may not interfere with any future additions to the house, if the surrounding property should hereafter tempt its possessor to give it more importance of Character. The Situation must be considered as plain, and of course very distant views are not to be expected; but there are many objects which it would be wrong to exclude, and if the plantations which are necessary (almost everywhere) to hide the pale, be kept low as copse-wood they will become excellent nurserys for game, and answer the expectation of the Sportsman better than lofty woods.

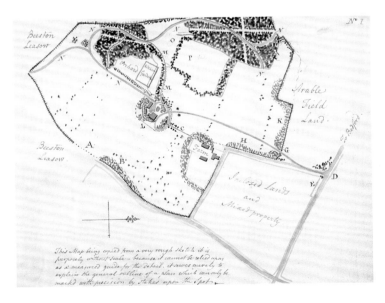

fig. 7 Repton, Red Book for 'Mogenhanger' 1792, plan of proposals (see fig. 16 page 33 for a larger version). Repton's new drive comes in from the Bedford road (right), G is the site for the lodge, and his proposals for screening carefully guide the views. The old drive of Muggerhanger Lodge is turned into a pleasure drive (to the left) to a view to Northill church, and other drives and walks are taken through the woods. Repton's views and walks are implicit in the restoration scheme.

Is Repton openly admitting that he finds no interest in this site, secretly saying to himself 'Whatever can I do to improve this?' But on future reflection he sets out his proposals without much alteration to a small estate by underplaying his scheme so that Godfrey Thornton will find it easy to approve, leaving it to Repton to supervise in his absence. He finds much that is not satisfactory (fig. 7).

Repton commences first with his concern with the views from the dining room ending with advice on how the land from the house should move from a grass lawn near the house and lead to a park followed by fields for arable farming – in case Mr Thornton is unaware of the progression of land away from the house to the wider landscape:

> I have frequently had occasion to observe, that the view from the dining room, is of all apartments that which is of the least consequence; but as in this case the dining room will also be a breakfast parlour, and perhaps the general living room of the family, it will require more attention. At present, the park-pale meets the eye immediately and beyond it is the Beeston Leasows, as the ground in the park falls from the eye and that of the Leasows rises again, the latter will always be the more conspicuous, and if it could ever be in corn it will be very injurious to the scene; I hope therefore it will not be impossible to obtain that part of the Leasows immediately opposite, and that it will always be preserved in grass.

He next moves on to the views from the drawing room (figs. 5 and 6) criticising Soane's internal planning of the house:

> There is difficulty in the management of this view, from the drawing-room window being placed so near to the door of the house; because it is almost impossible to preserve an air of neatness under the windows of a drawing room (especially when they are so very low) while the hall door requires an expanse of gravel for coaches to turn upon, and is exposed to the occasional defilement of Horses waiting at the door, and immediately under the windows. I am aware that the disposition of the rooms was not a matter of choice at Moggerhanger, such inconveniences being often unavoidable where Genius is confined to altering of an old house, instead of having full latitude to plan a new one; but it is necessary for me to explain the inconveniences arising from the proximity of the drawing room and the Entrance.
>
> I propose that the road shall pass in the form of a neat gravel drive under the drawing room window to the door, and return by a sweep at some distance behind a shrubbery, and close to the light fence which encloses a portion of dressed ground near the house.
>
> Immediately in front of the door is an avenue, from which a few trees might

fig. 8 Repton's Supplement to his Red Book, titled Beeston Leasows, 1798; he was very conscious of the view to the south from the house, marred by an offending cornfield, and suggests sinking the park fence to make the vista continuous, buying the fields (which Godfrey Thornton did) and so setting the view 'at perfect liberty' to enrich the lawn. He further suggested building a Cottage 'coming forward on the brow of the hill' to appropriate the view to Moggerhanger's house; Repton hoped that the cottage would be ornamented with shrubs and the door and windows painted green, 'so that it may not appear the humble habitation of a poor Labourer but rather the reward of some favourite Servant, made comfortable by the elegant attention of the Ladies'.

perhaps be taken away to advantage, but as their total removal would only show so much more of the farm buildings, I think it will be advisable to hide the stems of the trees by some plantation of flowering shrubs, which serves to conceal the return road for coaches, and part of the fence. From hence also may be a convenient path leading to the farm house under the shade of the trees. I trust there will be no doubt of the necessity for removing the two stagnated pools of muddy water.

One such pool was near the drawing room window, which if it remained a coach and horse would splash water on to the window. While spending much attention on minor alterations Repton does advise in detail about the Approach, commencing with improvements to the village.

Was he advising Godfrey Thornton if you want to live the role as a local landowner one should give the impression that you own the houses of the workers on your estate, and the best way of dealing with them is as follows? He advised using evergreens and climbing plants to improve the village scene at Moggerhanger, but cannot avoid a further comment about the relation of the house to the farm following Soane's improvements:

> Nothing contributes more to the importance of a place, than the appearance of neatness and attention to the comforts of the neighbouring poor; a village in good repair without any uniformity, except the same kind of pale to all the gardens, and the houses being grouped with a few Spruce firs and Laurels to hide the more shabby or dirty parts of them, gives a pleasing impression to the mind, and is infinitely more compatible with true taste, than the vain and extravagant rage for uninterrupted domain that suggests the idea of destroying villages and depopulating Towns, an idea too fatally prevalent in the neighbourhood of modern places. The houses in Moggerhanger parish are already in very neat repair, they only want a few honeysuckles or vines to decorate their walls, and some evergreen trees to unite and combine the several detached buildings.
>
> The farmhouse is at present too important in its position for the mansion, indeed it is the principal object of the two; and I think the best way to remedy this defect, without planting out the view from its windows, will be to cover the walls with vines or pear trees, which will serve to make it more picturesque, and also render it more subordinate in the general scenery (fig. 9).

For a park devoid of any eye-catchers in the surrounding landscape, Repton found little to include in his scheme except a long view back to the greensand ridge on which stands his other client's property Hazells Hall:

> It is a very common error to mistake what are the proper objects of beauty in

fig. 9 Repton, Supplement to his Red Book 1798, these *before* and *after* sketches showing the ornamentation of a façade were difficult to identify, thought to have been for Park Farm, but now accepted as his suggested scheme for the south, garden, front of the house, which John Soane could not accept.

distant scenery, and it is this error which so frequently does injury to the views in a park, by indiscriminately clearing away hedges to show objects that do not repay us when they are introduced: such are generally speaking the distant views of many church steeples and windmills, and objects may sometimes be singly introduced in those little peeps thro' a thicket in the course of a walk where it is usual to place a bench to attract the notice of a careless observer; but few village churches at a mile distant are in themselves objects of beauty: it must be by their accompaniments that they become such, either from the harmonious assemblage of a few houses around them, or the picturesque forms of shrubs with which the tower is grouped, and combines into one pleasing whole; perhaps a knoll crowned by trees out of which rises 'the heaven directed spire' or the mantling Ivy creeping up the massive tower and that too 'embossom'd high in Tufted trees'. These are objects worthy of our selection, but whether we see five, or five score Churches, which look no better than barns, can be no object of rational enquiry.

The little corner of Hasells-hall embosomed in its venerable woods, is doubtless the finest distant object that can be obtained in Moggerhanger park. The Woods are truly magnificent and worthy of every effort to introduce them to advantage. I think it may be effected by leading one of the walks thro' the thicket in such a direction, that the distant wood shall present itself.

John Byng undertook a later tour of the county in 1794, starting in Biggleswade. On 1 May he comments: 'The soil is very dry and the views very beautiful, but rain is wanted by the farmer and the rider.' Monday, 12 May, he passes Moggerhanger 'Having a wish to see what alterations and improvements Mr T[hornton] was making at Moggerhanger we rode 3 miles further to that place which is truly a dismal hopeless spot where Mr T[hornton] has spent much money but which the best taste, and the first fortune can never bring to beauty or comfort, and it wants water, soil and timber.'

On 19/20 May he records:

> Passing through the neighbourhood of Southill any observer would be astonished at the culture and gardening of the fields; surpassing everything I ever saw, for every field is cropped by peas, carrots, parsnips, French beans, cucumbers etc., etc., even the very open fields; and you cannot prevent your horse from smashing the cucumbers.
>
> Passing by the end of Beeston hamlet you come to Girford Bridge (over the Ivel) newly built with sandstone. To the left is the newly repaired house of Mr T(hornton) upon the hill at Muggerhanger; and in front, upon the river, the steeple of Blunham church – surrounded by the cultivation before mentioned – Sandy fields exhibit the same shew of fertility. To the right, upon the hill, amidst woods, stands the new built seat of Mr Pym.

Thomas Stone, land surveyor of Gray's Inn was sent to look at Bedfordshire by the newly formed Board of Agriculture. He published his *General View of the Agriculture of the County of Bedford* in 1794 and his report, although very critical of the state of agriculture at the time, included the following observations:

> The County of Bedfordshire though so near the Metropolis, is not remarkable for the excellence of its agriculture or attention to its breed of cattle or sheep. The climate is mild and genial, and favourable to the growth of corn and vegetables. Its surface is diversified by the hills and vales, and by nature, there is no district in the island better adapted for improvements.
>
> The one principal cause of this delay in the improvement of the agriculture of this county, has been the inattention, which, till of late, gentlemen of landed property, have shewn towards the advancement in rural economy, and to improvement in a science in which they are so materially interested [had he by any chance seen what Byng had witnessed at Southill?].
>
> On the whole, if under the patronage of so valuable an institution as the Board of Agriculture, proper measures were speedily taken for the improvements of the County of Bedfordshire, there can be no doubt that in the space of a very few years the population of the county would be considerably increased, the situation of every individual in it would be materially bettered, and the Kingdom at large would receive a very important accession to its opulence and strength.

WOBURN ABBEY

Towards the end of the 1790s the 5th Duke of Bedford carried out major changes to his vast estate, 3,000 acre park and house at Woburn Abbey and moved into what became his major residence after the demolition of his London home Bedford House in 1800. Within a short time Woburn became not only a showpiece in Bedfordshire but also in the whole country. This move into the country was copied by other successful merchants and businessmen, including his political ally Sam Whitbread who bought the 10,000 acre Southill estate in 1795. Both the duke and Mr Whitbread employed Henry Holland as their architect, who produced landscaping plans to accompany his new gallery and Chinese dairy at Woburn.

The 6th Duke of Bedford continued his father's interest in the new estate and immediately in 1803 introduced innovations ranging from forestry to sheep shearing and model farms. But he also became particularly interested in promoting horticulture as a science, using his new gardens near the house. Joseph Banks had promoted the scientific importance of botany and in order to achieve this the duke gathered at Woburn notable botanists who conducted experiments in his new glasshouses which were the latest in glass technology. Among others who came to Woburn were eminent chemists and also the landscape gardener Humphry Repton. Woburn quickly entered the ranks of other progressive aristocratic estates, such as Syon in Middlesex, Chatsworth in Derbyshire and Harewood in Yorkshire.

Repton's first visit to Woburn was in 1804. His Red Book was presented to the duke in January 1805. To impress the duke, Repton's Red Book contained ninety pages and forty-seven drawings, a map and diagrams including Repton's own fine watercolours and illustrated proposals. He suggests altering the drive of the London approach to the house to pass a new stretch of water, opening up the view to the house which stands on a slight rise in the park.

Repton, who has quickly grasped what the duke is attempting, immediately states he thinks Hollands's plantings are not what is required. 'I must condemn what Mr Holland has done at Woburn as a Landscape Gardener.' Holland had little landscape experience or expertise, even though he was Capability Brown's son-in-law and sometime collaborator. In the accounts it would appear that Repton took charge of the landscaping and collaborated with Holland. It was obviously politic to do so. The Red Book refers to earlier excavations on the site and excites the duke's historical interest. He combines this with the duchess's interest in plants and produced a scheme in which he concentrated on connecting the various buildings into a whole forming an extensive 'Pleasure Grounds'.

Using the horticultural science encouraged at Woburn, Repton planned an arboretum, an American garden, a Chinese garden around the dairy, a rosary and a menagerie garden making the whole a formal Pleasure Garden. He planted recently introduced shrubs and roses including *Hydrangea macrophylla* and *Aucuba japonica* and the repeat flowering Chinese rose.

At Woburn rather than any other estate in the country Repton established his horticultural reputation. He wrote 'The Improvements I have had the honour to suggest have nowhere been fully realised as at Woburn Abbey.' He was paid a retaining fee of £1,000 per annum by the duke, way above the 5 guineas he charged other clients like Mr Thornton. Sadly by 1833 some of his designs had been changed to suit the duke's botanical requirements.

Warseley Park (Huntingdonshire)

In spring 1792 Humphry Repton was asked to advise William Needham Esq. on improvements to his park. John Byng had word of this and had noted the fact in his diary, commenting in 1794 that 'Mr Needham who lives at Waresley wastes his life in solitary illness; surely fortune can find friends or entice companions?' The Red Book was produced on 30 May 1792; again we see Repton's speed in producing one. It is likely that his proposals were not immediately carried out as William died in 1806 leaving Waresley Park to Francis Needham. The frontispiece in the Red Book was amended so it now read 'Waresley Park . . . A Seat of the late William Needham Esq., and Francis Earl and Viscount Killmorey.'

Originally Warseley was a deer park, situated like The Hazells on the edge of the greensand ridge on undulating ground. Repton began: 'The great age and size of the many venerable trees scattered about Waresley Park, cannot fail to confer on the place an air of importance and antiquity, however it may be counteracted by the motley appearance of the house and the limited extant of the Lawn, arising from the boundary everywhere presenting itself.'

Repton thought the park could be improved by concealing the boundaries and removing many of the park palings and the planting of new trees. 'I propose to stop the deer from going quite present, round the house as they do at present. The new trees and plantation are necessary to hide offices, stables, kitchen garden and to connect them with each other.'

He recommended changing from a 'nondescript Grecian style to a "*Gothic*" Appearance'. Francis Needham chose the Grecian option for the house which gave it an elevation reminiscent of a factory. It was pulled down in 1834 by Charles Duncombe the new owner who died soon after in 1841.

Repton at Wimpole

Humphry Repton made two visits to the large estate of the Earls of Hardwicke at Wimpole in Cambridgeshire, in July and September 1801, and his Red Book was speedily completed and delivered in November of the same year. The speed by which he produced his Red Books at this time would suggest he no longer surveyed the grounds of each commission himself, now relying on the use of maps of the period. He is thought to have copied an existing map, 'A Map of the PARK, Pleasure grounds and HOME FARM at WIMPOLE', for his Wimpole proposals. He travelled directly from Hare Street, via Royston, to Wimpole, staying the night with the Hardwickes, thus avoiding the need of an inn.

Earlier in 1792 Repton produced a Red Book for Port Eliot in Cornwall. It was while working on these proposals, Repton was recommended to relatives of the family. The 1st Baron Edward Craggs-Eliot was related by marriage to the step-sister of the 3rd Earl of Hardwicke.

Following in the footsteps of Lancelot Brown whose scheme for the 2nd Earl, constructing the lakes to the north of Wimpole's park, had been newly planted with 6,403 trees obtained by James Wood's nursery at Huntingdon, only a few of Repton's proposals were carried out. However, Repton proposed the removal of some trees 'by the judicious use of the axe', although he argued that by the removal of some hundred trees 'the place would be made to appear more wooded'.

Repton suggested a flower garden between the projecting library and the laundry wings enclosed by railing with a central gate flanked by piers surmounted by stone vases, which is a somewhat new solution to what he had earlier avoided. (Although not actually carried out, this solution became the idea for a later scheme carried out in the mid-nineteenth century). A marginal note in the Red Book that may be in the hand of his patron states: 'Expensive and the appearance doubtful.' He also proposed a more natural treatment to the banks of Brown's lakes, and planting around the Hill House which had been built to the west of the main house on rising land.

He argued that as the house was 'totally hid from trees' from the main west drive but 'the stables were immediately brought into view', that by a slight adjustment to the route of the drive 'the house is seen just so much in front as to shew that it consists of a centre and two wings'. Repton again improved the importance of the house when approached by a visitor.

Repton's proposals for a row of brick cottages to the north of John Soane's model farm included a timber verandah supporting a trellised connection to the roof, with vines to soften the elevation and the white framed windows of the upper storey painted in a softer colour. These could have easily have been as suggested for Thornton's cottages in the village of Moggerhanger. Repton was asked to return to Wimpole in 1809 to create a new glazed conservatory on the site of an earlier seventeenth-century orangery to the west of the house.

Market Gardening and Agriculture in Bedfordshire

By 1880 corn production in the county was the main cash crop. If wheat prospered, the agricultural community prospered, and so would Bedfordshire as a whole. In 1867 the price of wheat was 64s. 5d. per quarter but by 1884 the price had declined to 35s. 8d. a quarter, due to very poor summers and the import of cheaper grain from America. Similarly the price of barley declined after the repeal of the Malt Tax in 1830. In the 1860s this decline spelt disaster to a county so dependent on agriculture.

Some farmers changed from arable to meat and milk production, but only on a smaller scale, slowly increasing until 1894 when more farmers abandoned wheat following further wet summers. One suggestion to stop the decline of prices was to turn to market gardening, but this was only possible on the lighter lands between Biggleswade and Sandy. But at the start any profit was reduced by high freight costs imposed by the Great North Railway. Local farmers found it difficult to compete in the capital with market gardeners from Middlesex. One farmer declared 'market gardening is all humbug and nonsense. Why the markets are always glutted with garden produce now, and how can strong clay be gardened?'

To reduce the impact of lower prices some landlords reduced their tenants' rent. The Duke of Bedford reduced his rent nine times between 1879 and 1889 sometimes allowing half the annual rent to be waived. The Pym estate was helped by substantial rents from their central London property; the estate had had some valuable market garden land in addition to heavier land. The estate steward, a Mr C. W. Preedy, tried with no success to raise market garden rents in 1875. The *Bedfordshire Mercury* stated: 'The well known honour of Mr Pym's family and the consideration to good tenants for many years past, encouraged this system of cultivation, and affordable reliable security to the tenants for their profits. It is therefore the general astonishment and disapproval; that notice came from a new agent recently appointed in place of Alexander Pym, of a sudden rise of £1 or even £2 per acre, after an alternative note to quit.' This was quickly dropped and the estate settled to management on more acceptable lines. To balance this problem Pym managed to raise his London rents by 74 per cent in 1890.

In 1871 Biggleswade was the 3rd largest town in Bedfordshire. It was badly hit by the agricultural depression. Between 1877 and 1914 two-thirds of businesses disappeared, many market gardeners, builders, umbrella makers, harness makers, corn factors, and even agricultural implement makers all ceased to trade. This general decline surrounded the *very* specific downfall of the Moggerhanger estate; but even so, in a plan of 1917 (fig. 10) for the sale of the parkland in lots, many of the features of Repton's approach had survived.

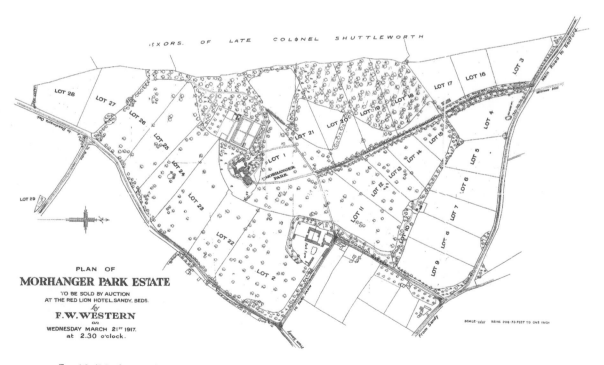

fig. 10 'Morhanger' Park Estate 1917 plan for sale of the park in 28 Lots for market gardening;
Lot 1, the Park house and Garden Wood was acquired by Bedfordshire County Council.

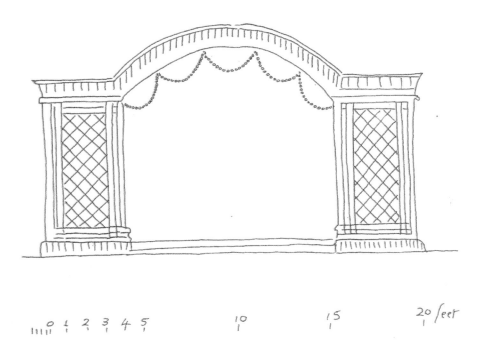

fig. 11 Moggerhanger Park, proposed alcove seat, John Drake after Repton, Red Book 1798.

Sources

Adshead, David, *Wimpole: Architectural Drawings and Topographical Views*, London, 2007.

Batchelor, Thomas, *General View of the Agriculture of the County of Bedford*, London, 1808.

Byng, John, *The Torrington Diaries 1781–1794*, ed. C. Bruyn Andrews, 3 vols., 1938.

Cambridgeshire Gardens Trust, *The Gardens of Cambridgeshire: A Gazetteer*, St Neots, 2000.

Collett-White, James, *Bedfordshire in the 1880s*, Bedford, n.d.

Daniels, Stephen, *Humphry Repton: Landscape Gardening and the Geography of Georgian England*, New Haven, CT, 1999.

Drake, John, *Wood & Ingram: A Huntingdonshire Nursery 1742–1950*, Huntingdon, 2008.

Jack, Eleanor, 'Humphry Repton and the Red Book of Waresley', Cambridgeshire Gardens Trust Collection.

Repton, 'Mogenhanger' Red Book 1792, National Archives/English Heritage [copy], Lois Hunt Red Book Collection, Heveningham Hall, Suffolk.

Repton, Supplement (Beeston Leasowes) 1798, BL RP 5265 [copy], Lois Hunt Red Book Collection, Heveningham Hall, Suffolk.

Pym, Francis, *Sentimental Journey: Tracing an Outline of Family History*, Sandy, Beds, 1998.

Stone, Thomas, *General View of the Agriculture of the County of Bedford*, London, 1794.

Previous page: George Garrard, 'Woburn Sheep Shearing', 1804: the 6th Duke of Bedford is sitting on his horse in the centre; the group at the bottom right watching the shearers at work consists of Arthur Young (with notebook), talking to Sir John Sinclair, Sir Joseph Banks (seated) and Thomas W. Coke – though the standing figure to the right may be Godfrey Thornton.

PIETY AND PLUTOCRACY:
THE SOCIAL AND BUSINESS WORLD
OF THE THORNTONS

GARETH ATKINS

SIX

Bad news always unsettles the financial markets. 'Yesterday morning,' reported newspapers on Friday 19 August 1814, 'the Stock Exchange was thrown into a state of dismay by the declaration, that a person of some consideration in the City had confessed himself unable or unwilling to pay his differences, to the amount of £45,000.'[1] Details emerged over the next few days. The 'person' at the centre of the scandal was Robert Thornton, an MP, leading London businessman, intimate of the Prince Regent and chairman of the Honourable East India Company. This, then, was no ordinary bankruptcy. Yet the story was depressingly familiar: finding himself in financial difficulties, in recent years Thornton had resorted to speculation in order to maintain a lavish lifestyle at his Clapham residence. 'At first he was very successful and gained £30,000 or £40,000,' his sister-in-law told a friend.

> This very success proved fatal, for enamoured of his own sagacity he went on venturing more and more, till the depression in the stocks annihilated all his gains and in the true spirit of a gambler he attempted to retrieve this loss by desperate efforts and at last foiled and disappointed in every effort he became a defaulter to the amount of £45,000.[2]

This was an immense sum – worth perhaps £30m in today's terms – and the ensuing sale of his famous library, his collection of prints and other property failed to satisfy Thornton's creditors.[3] As comments in the newspapers built to a crescendo, his nerve broke. By September he was in France, living under an assumed name, and in the turmoil surrounding the return of Napoleon in early

THORNTON, SMITH, STEPHEN, SUMNER, SYKES AND WILBERFORCE FAMILIES

This family tree charts major relationships. Some spouses and children are not shown.

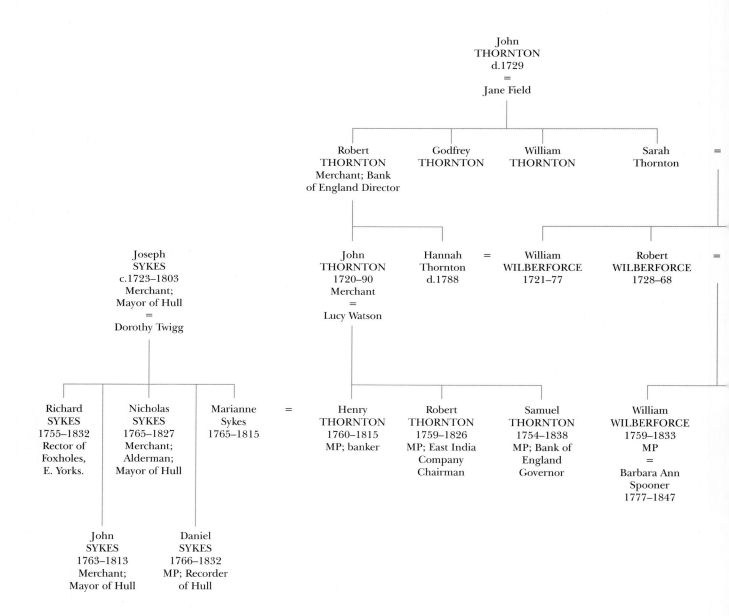

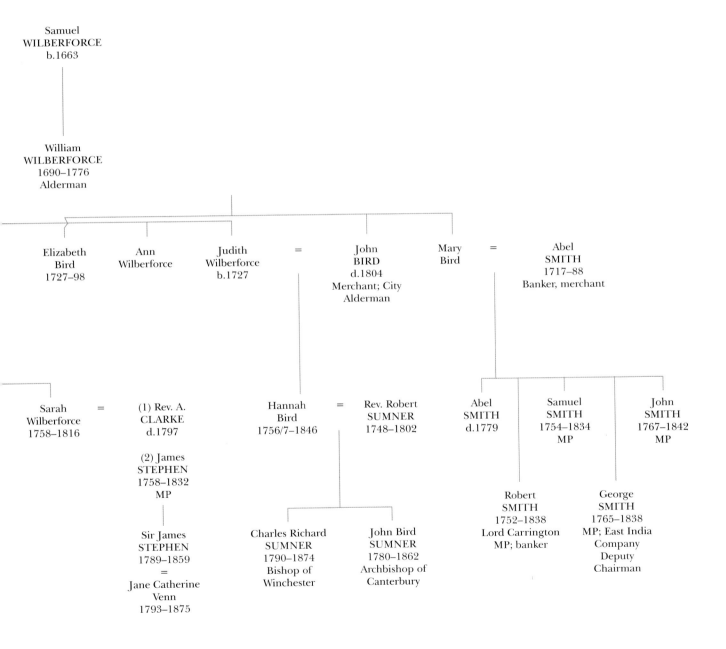

1815 'Richard Tyler' fled to the United States.[4] He died there in 1826. Though they had long pursued different ends, mused his brother Henry sadly, 'I had never till now had to contemplate him as a Prodigal who had literally wandered from home.'[5]

What made Robert's fall all the more shocking was a widespread sense that this was not the behaviour expected of a Thornton. According to the *Gentleman's Magazine* his father, John (1720–90), had been 'the greatest merchant in Europe, except Mr. Hope, of Amsterdam', and, despite giving to charity between £100,000 and £150,000 during his lifetime, had left an estate valued at £600,000.[6] Robert (1759–1826) and his brothers, Samuel (1754–1838) and Henry (1760–1815), were known to be heirs to a vast commercial empire that stretched from Hull and London to St Petersburg and the Baltic, which dealt in everything from sugar and soap refining to shipping, tar, timber and cordage. They enjoyed links with other late eighteenth-century merchant dynasties – the Wilberforces, Watsons and Sykeses of the Thorntons' native Hull, not to mention major bankers like the Smiths of Nottingham and London – which were cemented by marriage alliances as well as business collaboration.[7] (See family tree pp.186–187).

With interests covering much of the east coast and Midlands, this nexus was highly prosperous, and through associates at Westminster it could also boast appreciable political clout. But although profit and influence were all well and good, this was also a world in which trust was paramount. Personal sobriety and rectitude were cardinal virtues among London's merchantocracy. Small wonder, then, that Robert's disgrace caused such a stir. Family disapproval still echoes through the pages of *Marianne Thornton*, E. M. Forster's famous memoir of his great aunt, published over a hundred years later in 1956.

All this provides important background against which to consider the owners and improvers of Moggerhanger Park. For despite the fact that Godfrey Thornton (1737–1805) and his sons Stephen (1767–1850) and William (1774–1847) were men of substance both in the City of London and in Bedfordshire, we have tantalisingly little evidence of what they were really like. We know, for instance, that from 1772–1801 Godfrey occupied one of the twenty-four prestigious directorships of the Bank of England, being deputy-governor from 1791–3 then governor from 1793–5; and we know also that he was High Sheriff of Bedfordshire from 1803–4. His sons became partners in the family business and followed similar paths, Stephen as director at the Bank and High Sheriff in his turn, and William as MP and director of the East India Company.

But aside from a few likenesses and some unrevealing scattered letters, no personal effects survive. The family memorials in Blunham church are monotonously formulaic: Godfrey was apparently 'an excellent man' and 'most kind parent'. And although Moggerhanger itself is ample proof of their taste, wealth and status, it too gives little away. What we do know, however, is that Godfrey Thornton and his sons were part of an extended cousinhood which carried not just considerable influence in pre-Victorian high finance but – more famously – played a leading part in the political and philanthropic affairs of the age. Known derisively as the 'Saints', William Wilberforce, Henry Thornton and their allies in Parliament spearheaded reforming endeavours at

Westminster and further afield, most famously the campaign for the abolition of the slave trade.[8] Members of the group – later labelled the 'Clapham Sect' – presided over numerous philanthropic committees; they headed countless printed subscription lists; they assumed prominent places on the platforms at anniversary meetings as of right. In short, the Moggerhanger Thorntons were part of a world in which piety and plutocracy went hand-in-hand. What follows aims to reconstruct that world and their place in it.

PIETY AND PLUTOCRACY

The phenomenon now known as the 'Evangelical Revival' was well under way by 1750. But it was only in the closing decades of the eighteenth century that this combination of heartfelt religiosity, conversionism and fervent activism began to make its mark on the upper echelons of British society. Amid a national mood of soul-searching prompted by the recent loss of America, the 1780s and 90s witnessed a widespread upsurge in moral reformism. This temper was especially pronounced among bankers and businessmen, whose exposure to the frequent financial crises that punctuated the period (1788, 1793, 1797, 1803, 1807–8, 1810–11, 1816, 1819, 1820 and 1826) kept apprehensions of failure at fever pitch. Indeed, the sheer volatility of the market convinced many that the intervening hand of Providence was at work. One banker interpreted the 1820 Dublin crash as 'the judgment of the Lord passing through the Land'. 'To see the waters gradually rising, the mountains and strongholds of commercial credit one after another overwhelmed in the mighty flood . . . brought the feeling home to ourselves – "What are we more than others?"'[9] Such attitudes were increasingly common among evangelicals, who consoled themselves with the idea that such catastrophes were sent by God for moral purification. 'Business has often been productive of trial to me, and has led me to reflect on the equity of God, who measures out His salutary chastisements, even in this world, to the rich as well as the poor,' mused the Quaker J. J. Gurney.[10]

Perhaps predictably, given the turbulence of the times, contemporary businessmen placed a high premium on projecting an image of unflappability. J. H. Tritton's 'extreme caution, inflexible integrity and firmness . . . punctuality and self-command' sent one Barclays colleague into raptures.[11] Henry Thornton was clear on this point. 'I consider myself to possess as a Banker the character in a great measure of a trustee to our customers,' he informed a business partner. 'I, as elder partner,' he added, '. . . am counted on as a guarantee that all is safe.'[12]

The moral earnestness of the moneyed orders was reflected in their attitudes to wealth. For although this was a period of burgeoning prosperity for investors, this was not always cause for rejoicing. Far from it: many serious-minded businessmen saw their fortunes as a worrisome and potentially corrupting burden. Their fears about the lure of Mammon were lent shape by a succession of luridly publicised fraud scandals. One of the most lurid was also uncomfortably close to home for the Thorntons, originating as it did at the London headquarters of their cousins' firm, Smith, Payne and Smiths. News of the suicide of their confidential clerk, William Hancock, in January 1807, doubtless came as an unpleasant surprise. 'When this reaches your hand,' read a macabre letter of confession addressed to his employers, 'mine will be lifeless.'[13] The plot thickened, however, when they opened Hancock's desk. His papers revealed that over the preceding twenty-seven years their trusted employee had robbed them of enormous sums of money. More chilling still was the discovery of unsent letters going back as far as 1798 wherein he confessed the enormity of his sins, referring to 'infernal' temptations and the 'evil genius' he acted under. Only after his defalcations reached the staggering total of £87,800 had his nerve broken.[14] Most bizarrely of all, no one could fathom why he had done it. Such details helped to reinforce the sense that money in itself was a potent snare for the unwary. The growing purchase of this idea helps to account, for example, for an increasing antipathy in these circles towards gambling. That the Smiths deemed a loss *or* a gain of twenty pounds in a day at the gaming table sufficient grounds for breaking with a partner should not surprise us.[15] After all, money was held in trust as a gift from God. And whether invested or given away, it was to be stewarded with the utmost responsibility. This was why many, like John Thornton and his sons, gave away such large proportions of their income to charity; and it also explains why they spent so much space in diaries and memoranda agonising over whom to give it to.

If psychological and spiritual pressures prompted many businessmen to consider eternal things, it was natural that they should come to regard religion as a prophylactic against fraud and unreliability. Such motivations were almost certainly behind the employment of one George Moore, brought in from London by Smiths to clean out the 'Augean stable' of their Lincoln branch after an embezzlement scandal in 1792. The fact that his employers set great store by religious belief also accounts, on the other hand, for the dismissal of William Christmas by Hoares Bank in 1825. 'His sentiments are known to be radical and I fear no religious principles are guiding or protecting his slippery path,' remarked the evangelical head of the house, Henry Hoare.[16]

Admittedly, pious businessmen were often too easily impressed by empty words: Henry Thornton's diary frequently evinces his disillusionment at being let down by self-professed Christians who ought to have known better. Nevertheless, this did not stop him from making unsuccessful but repeated efforts to convert his long-suffering banking partners at Down, Thornton and Free. Does all this mean that Godfrey Thornton and his sons shared the faith of their more famous Clapham cousins? Not necessarily. While Henry Thornton spent two years at the beginning of his career in his uncle's counting house, his autobiographical 'Recollections' give only the barest details.[17] Yet much can be surmised. Although personal probity had always been highly valued, the Moggerhanger Thorntons inhabited a world which was fast becoming infused with a more overtly evangelical flavour. As the next section will show, this was to have considerable practical significance.

EVANGELICALS AND THE CITY

While the influence of the Saints at Westminster is well known, it is often forgotten that their real power base lay at the other end of London, in the narrow streets of the financial Square Mile. 'We are all City people and connected with merchants, and nothing but merchants on every side,' Henry Thornton once remarked.[18] The Thorntons and Smiths, as we have seen, formed an especially closely knit nexus, but by the 1800s and 1810s there were numerous other families – the Barclays, Deacons, Drummonds, Grotes, Hoares, Mannings, Neales, Raikeses and Williamses being some of the most prominent – who were strongly tinged with serious religion.[19] Even Sir Thomas Baring, one of the heirs to mighty Barings Bank – the 'sixth great power in Europe' – was a close friend and ally of Wilberforce. Henry Thornton's firm was based at Bartholomew Lane, in the shadow of the Bank of England, and it is worth making clear that when he spoke at Westminster, he frequently did so on behalf of the City. His election as member for Southwark, moreover, owed a great deal to the influence he could command north of the river. 'I think he must have been thrown out but for the exertions of his friends in the City . . . in the India House etc.,' his wife told a friend in 1807.[20] Other Saints too were banking members, including Thomas Babington, Charles Barclay and the four La Touche brothers, David, John, Peter and Robert. One of the most prominent was Samuel Thornton, whose influence as confidant of the Chancellor of the Exchequer, and as director and later governor of the Bank of England, was well known. It would appear that Samuel was far from acting alone: indeed, by 1817 'A Constant Reader' felt so strongly about misplaced religiosity at Threadneedle Street that he complained to the *Morning Chronicle*.[21] Likely targets of his ire included Henry Manning, Edward Simeon, Richard Mee Raikes and of course Stephen Thornton (director 1802–20). Given the pious complexion of the Bank, it is significant that its solicitor, J.W. Freshfield, was also prominent as an outspoken defender of the evangelical-led British and Foreign Bible Society.[22]

Phobias about the malign spread of evangelical influence were even more pronounced when it came to the East India Company, whose headquarters was in nearby Leadenhall Street. For critics like Sydney Smith, the grandiose neo-classical façade of East India House masked a teeming hive of pious place-finders eager to promote their co-religionists. 'Methodism at home is no unprofitable game to play,' he sneered. 'In the East it will soon be the infallible road to promotion.'[23] In fairness to Smith, there was much truth in this. Indeed, since the East India stock which so many evangelical bankers and merchants held conferred the right to vote in elections to the Court of Directors, it was hardly surprising that they should seek to influence the affairs of the Company. Close associates of the Saints – Charles Grant, Edward Parry, George Smith and Robert Thornton – dominated elections for its chairmanship and deputy-chairmanship during the 1800s and 1810s. It was with these friends and relations that Godfrey's other son allied himself. Taking the name Astell in 1807 in order to inherit the estates of his maternal grandmother, William was MP for forty years and a director for forty-six. Whether or not he was, as another director sourly put it, a 'vain empty blockhead totally unequal to the situation', many suspected that he was little more than the puppet of the powerful Charles Grant.[24] Lord Teignmouth – Governor-General of Bengal from 1793–8 and member of the Indian Board of Control from 1807 – was another ally. The emergence of this power bloc came at a critical time, for in the aftermath of the Vellore Mutiny in 1806 questions were being asked about whether missions had a destabilising influence. Grant, Parry and their cronies, fumed one contemporary, would 'march from Clapham Common (fig. 1) to overturn the religion of all India' for the sake of a handful of native converts.[25] The eventual passing of the 'Pious Clause' in 1813,

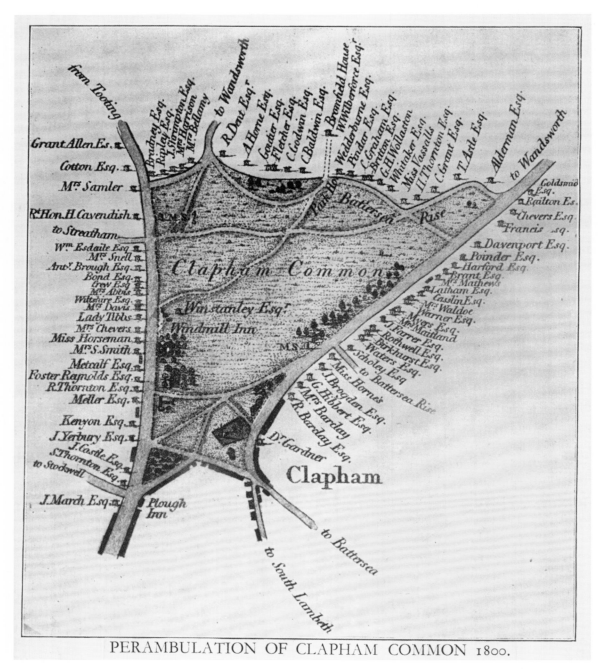

PERAMBULATION OF CLAPHAM COMMON 1800.

fig. 1 *Perambulation of Clapham Common, 1800.* Note the houses of Samuel and Robert Thornton on the western side, of William Wilberforce, Henry Thornton, Charles Grant and William Thornton Astell in the north, and other banking families (Esdaile, Goldsmid, Harford, Barclay) close by.

whereby Parliament decreed that missionaries *should* be allowed into Company possessions, was one of the Saints' signal triumphs. That the measure succeeded was due to a cleverly orchestrated petitioning campaign, but the part played by those within the Company should not be underestimated. Evangelicals would retain behind-the-scenes influence in colonial affairs for many decades to come.

Like many nouveaux riches, such men were by no means averse to displaying their wealth. In fact, it might be argued that this was part of their evangelistic strategy. Henry Thornton, for instance, was deeply critical of his more rough-hewn father's failure to cultivate the rich and influential. 'By becoming a little more respectable we become much more dangerous,' he declared.[26] His house at Battersea Rise was set in London's leafy Surrey suburbs amid the abodes of the *haute bourgeoisie*, and in the 1790s and 1800s it became a focus of well-heeled activism. Numerous schemes were hatched in its famous oval library, reputedly designed in an idle moment by William Pitt. Wilberforce, Grant and other like-minded luminaries took up residence nearby, not to mention the other Thornton brothers and their cousin, William Thornton Astell.[27] Such families enjoyed the finer things in life, and it is no coincidence that evangelically inclined

fig. 2 Blunham, SS Edmund and
James, Bacon's monument for
Godfrey Thornton, d. 1805.

artists like the painter Francis Rigaud, the pastel miniaturist John Russell and the sculptor John Bacon (fig. 2) became highly fashionable.[28] Like their Moggerhanger cousins, the Clapham Thorntons were also able and willing to pay for fine architecture. In 1800 Sir John Soane was called in to alter both Samuel's town residence at Old Broad Street and his new Surrey estate at Albury Park. The following year Soane was again at work, this time at Down, Thornton and Free.[29] Here as in Godfrey's case, the fact that Soane was the Bank's architect may well account for the choice, but it is tempting to speculate that Samuel and Henry might also have cast admiring glances towards the emerging masterpiece at Moggerhanger Park.

'THE AGE OF SOCIETIES'

Of course, there were limits as to how far such tastes should be indulged. That, at least, was Henry's opinion: although he thought little of spending £300 on a new coach before his marriage in 1796, he was ill at ease regarding his brothers' expensive ostentation. While Samuel's sumptuous dinner parties at Albury seemed to bespeak an unseemly desire to curry favour with the great and good, the vast sums squandered by Robert in creating his matchless Clapham garden and orangery did nothing to assuage Henry's mounting anxieties. Although his daughters were allowed to attend the glittering public breakfast Robert devised for Queen Charlotte in 1808, it was significant that Henry felt unable to attend in person.[30] One area in which lavish spending was *not* frowned upon, however, was philanthropy. Even after his marriage, when he curtailed his expenditure, Henry gave away roughly a third of his income annually. According to one calculation the Thorntons between them had 173 subscriptions to different charities.[31] This was impressive, but by no means was it exceptional. 'Ours is the age of societies,' wrote Sir James Stephen in a famous *Edinburgh Review* article. 'For the redress of every oppression that is done under the sun, there is a public meeting.'[32] Being the son of a Clapham family and married to

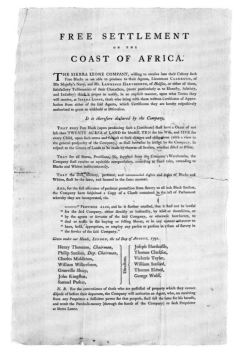

fig. 3 1791 Advertisement inviting 'Free Blacks' to settle at Sierra Leone.

the daughter of another, Stephen took care to ascribe much of the credit to his forebears. But even so, he had a point. The awesome energy that drove endeavours like the Bible Society, the missionary societies, the lying-in hospitals, the schools, the tract-giving, the relief funds, and above all the campaigns against Britain's slave trade, stemmed in large measure from the efforts of the Thorntons and others like them. This final section examines how they did it.

If finance fuelled the philanthropic boom of the late eighteenth and early nineteenth centuries, the shape it took owed much to the application of business acumen. Charitable activity was nothing new, but the scale and ambition of new concerns like the London Missionary Society (1795), Church Missionary Society (1799), Religious Tract Society (1799) and British and Foreign Bible Society (1804) marked a dramatic departure from the amateurish benevolent societies of earlier days. Employing full-time secretaries, corresponding committees and travelling fund-raisers, and based in permanent premises around the City, the newly founded societies looked more like transnational trading concerns than charitable organisations. The resemblance was heightened by the close involvement of businessmen in their day-to-day operations. They had numerous contacts both at home and abroad; they pioneered new printing technology in producing millions of Bibles and tracts as cheaply as possible; they boasted incomes of tens of thousands of pounds a year. Not for nothing did one commentator liken the proceedings of the Bible Society to those of the international shipping insurance-broker, Lloyd's.[33] One of the earliest and most explicit examples of the affinity between commerce and Christianity was the Sierra Leone Company (fig. 3), founded in 1791 by a consortium of Quaker and evangelical entrepreneurs to promote the resettlement of freed slaves in West Africa. From the outset it was clear that profit and philanthropy were to go hand-in-hand. In fact, in order to demonstrate to those in Britain that free labour was more efficient than forced labour, it was *paramount* that the Company make money for its shareholders. As it turned out, the Company had bitten off more than it could chew, and Sierra Leone instead became a Crown Colony in 1808. All the same, the idea that charities needed to be commercially savvy was to characterise the wave of new endeavours.

The Saints bore much of the burden of Sierra Leone affairs. 'I find that I can hardly keep an account of time,' Wilberforce wearily remarked at one point. 'H. Thornton has been at it the whole day for some months.'[34] In the 1790s and 1800s the drawing rooms of Clapham would also act as the headquarters of a successful national crusade against the slave trade. Such campaigns leant heavily on the oratory and appeal of the Saints' leader, William Wilberforce, and so when his re-election as MP for Yorkshire was contested in 1807, it was natural that his friends should rally round. Yet their task was undoubtedly tough: to stand any chance of success in a three-way battle against the mighty Fitzwilliam interest and the fortune of Henry Lascelles, Wilberforce needed money.

The ball was set rolling at a London meeting in May, and the resulting collection eventually realised nearly £65,000. Naturally the Claphamites were among the first to pledge their support, but subscription lists reveal contributions from across the financial and religious world.[35] Henry Thornton pledged £300, his brothers £100 apiece and the Hull banker Thomas Thompson no less than £500. (By this time Godfrey was dead, but Stephen Thornton, evidently approving of his cousin's politics, gave a sizeable £100.) Yet even this seemed inadequate. Henry Thornton and several friends hastened up the Great North Road to lend personal aid in what was becoming a gruelling poll. Supporters elsewhere could only take opium to calm their nerves and try to remain patient as they awaited news from the North.[36] After eighteen days of voting, the result was announced in early June.

It was a close-run thing. Wilberforce headed the poll with 11,808 votes, followed by Milton, 11,177, and Lascelles, 10,990. Evangelicals, anti-slavery enthusiasts and Wilberforce supporters of every stamp reacted with understandable jubilation. 'Your election has been honourable to the cause of religion,' rejoiced one friend, 'and I trust that our gracious God has again fixed you in your seat for great and good purposes.'[37] Maybe; but seeing as over £250,000 had been spent overall – making this the most expensive of any pre-1832 election – the success of Wilberforce's appeal had been a *sine qua non*.

One of the most laudable ways of spending money was to use it to ensure the preaching of the Gospel (fig. 4). In some ways this was a Thornton speciality: by exploiting the system whereby Church of England livings (i.e. the right to appoint a parish incumbent) were bought and sold, the patronage trust set up by John Thornton ensured a perpetual succession of 'Gospel Ministers' in several

fig. 4 'John Thornton giving Bibles to a Soldier and a Sailor', attributed to Edward Penney (1714–91). John Thornton died in 1790. Much of John Thornton's giving was done anonymously, but the provision of Bibles to the poor was one of his main priorities. He was a key supporter of one of the earliest evangelical tract-giving ventures, the Society for Promoting Religious Knowledge among the Poor, founded in 1750.

favoured places up and down the land. Inherited by Charles Simeon, the dynamic Vicar of Holy Trinity, Cambridge, the handful of Thornton parishes later became the nucleus of a more ambitious scheme to snap up fashionable pulpits in provincial centres – Bath, Cheltenham, Hull and the like. At the same time, however, there remained many individual patrons who also sought to appoint pious clergymen. Take Bedfordshire, for example, in around 1810. At Blunham, Stephen Thornton would have sat under the preaching of Robert Porten Beachcroft, a leading evangelical and protégé of Amabel Yorke, 5th Baroness Lucas. Within a few miles there was William Fancourt at Bletsoe and Melchbourne, appointed by the pious Lady St John; Richard Whittingham at Potton; and at Turvey, the bestselling author and preacher Legh Richmond. Looking just over the county boundary into Buckinghamshire, Olney had in the 1760s and 1770s been the home of John Newton, the ex-slaver and author of 'Amazing Grace', and was now thriving under Christopher Stephenson, appointed by the Earl of Dartmouth. Numerous other connections criss-crossed neighbouring counties.

What part did the Moggerhanger Thorntons play in all this? While John Thornton and the older Astells were intimates of the firebrand rector of Everton, John Berridge, in earlier years, there is no evidence that Godfrey Thornton shared their enthusiasms. We might imagine that he, like many of his peers, would have sniffed at the rough-edged revivalism of his cousins and their unconventional preacher. By the time Stephen Thornton inherited Moggerhanger in 1805, however, evangelicalism had mellowed, and so too had opinions of it among the great and good. So when we find Thornton and Beachcroft entertaining the tenants with dancing, fireworks and supper to celebrate George IV's coronation in 1821, it is reasonable to assume that the landowner and his rector were on good terms.[38] Henry Thornton, no doubt, would have approved.

Epilogue

Stephen Thornton died in 1850, and Moggerhanger passed out of Thornton hands seven years later. The cousinhood continued to produce clergymen, naval officers and, of course, bankers, but the Thorntons were never to have the same prominence they had enjoyed during the early decades of the century. This chapter has shown that they were part of an active, wealthy and richly varied cultural milieu. While strange in many respects, that milieu sometimes appears remarkably familiar: recent events suggest that modern policymakers would do well to heed the idea that morals and moneymaking go together. Yet more tangible legacies are few and far between. In Clapham, all that remains of the Thorntons is the orangery in which Robert dallied with royalty and titled guests. A more misleading memorial could hardly be conceived! Henry and his brothers may never have visited Moggerhanger Park. It is one of the sweeter ironies of history, then, that a house conceived by the less prominent branch of the family should stand today as its lasting monument.

NOTES

1. *Morning Chronicle*, 19 August 1814.
2. Taylor, Laurence and Thorne, R. G., 'Thornton, Robert' in *The House of Commons, 1790–1820*, v, p.375.
3. http://www.measuringworth.com/index.html
4. *The Examiner*, 28 Aug. 1814.
5. Diary, 6 Nov. 1814, Cambridge University Library, Thornton MSS, Add. 7674/1/R, ff.176–8.
6. *Gentleman's Magazine*, November 1790, 1056; Grayson Carter, 'John Thornton', in *Dictionary of English Biography*, vol. 2, pp.1103–4. Thornton's wife, Lucy Watson, was part of another Hull merchant dynasty.
7. One of the forerunners of Natwest.
8. The most extensive treatment is Ford K. Brown, *Fathers of the Victorians*, Cambridge, 1961; for a more recent rendering, see M. J. D. Roberts, *Making English Morals: Voluntary Association and Moral Reform in England, 1787–1886*, Cambridge, 2004, pp.17–142.
9. W. Urwick, *Biographic Sketches of James Digges La Touche Esq.*, Dublin, 1868, p.266.
10. Augustus J. C. Hare, *The Gurneys of Earlham*, 2 vols., London, 1895, vol. 2, pp.28–9.
11. Memorandum, Robert Barclay II, May 1833, cited in P. W. Matthews, *History of Barclays Bank Limited*, ed. A. W. Tuke, 2 vols., London, 1926, vol. 1, pp.41–2.
12. Henry Thornton to Peter Free, 10 June 1814, South Gyle, RBS Archives, Pole, Thornton, Free, Down and Scott MSS, PT 2/4.
13. J. A. S. L. Leighton-Boyce, *Smiths the Bankers 1658–1958*, London, 1958, p.134.
14. The fraud cost the equivalent of £55m at today's prices.
15. Leighton-Boyce, *Smiths*, p.142.
16. Cited in Victoria Hutchings, *Messrs Hoare Bankers: A History of the Hoare Banking Dynasty*, London, 2005, p.107. Henry Hoare (1750–1828) was a founder member of the Church Missionary Society and well-known charitable benefactor.
17. Henry Thornton, 'Recollections', Thornton MSS, Add 7674/1/N, f.15.
18. MS 'Recollections of Marianne Thornton' [1857], cited in Thornton, *Enquiry*, p.12.
19. Ian S. Rennie, 'Evangelicalism and English Public Life, 1823–1850', unpublished Ph.D. thesis, University of Toronto, 1962, p. 11; Hector Bolitho and Derek Peel, *The Drummonds of Charing Cross*, London, 1967, pp.137–44.
20. Mrs Henry Thornton to Hannah More, 11 May 1807, Thornton MSS, 'Family Letterbook', Add. 7674/1/N, f.229.
21. *Morning Chronicle*, 25 November 1817.
22. See Leslie Howsam, *Cheap Bibles: Nineteenth-Century Publishing and the British and Foreign Bible Society*, Cambridge, 1991, p.25. See also J.W. Freshfield, *Remarks on the 'Counter-Address' to the Inhabitants of Hackney, on the Proposed Formation of an Auxiliary Bible Society; and on a Paper Entitled 'Both Sides of the Question' &c. &c.*, London, 1812.
23. [Sydney Smith], *Extracts from the Edinburgh Review [Concerning Methodism]*, Edinburgh, 1810, pp.48–9.
24. H. V. Bowen, *The Business of Empire: The East India Company and Imperial Britain, 1756–1833*, Cambridge, 2000, p.137.
25. Thomas Grenville to Lord Grenville, 7 May 1813, cited in Ainslie T. Embree, *Charles Grant and British Rule in India*, London, 1962, p.273.
26. Henry Thornton to Hannah More, 26 January 1811, Thornton MSS, 'Family Letterbook', Add. 7674/1/N, f.286.
27. E. M. Howse, *Saints in Politics: The 'Clapham Sect' and the Growth of Freedom*, London, 1953, pp.15–27.
28. Doreen M. Rosman, *Evangelicals and Culture*, London, 1984, pp.158–62.
29. http://www.soane.org/soanebuildings.html. Last accessed 7 September 2010.
30. John William Grover, *Old Clapham: Based on a Lecture Delivered in the Year 1885 at the St Matthew's Church Institution and at the Clapham Hall*, London, 1887, p.66.
31. Brown, *Fathers*, p.358.
32. Sir James Stephen, *Essays in Ecclesiastical Biography*, 2 vols., London, 1849, vol. 2, 382.
33. John Shore, Lord Teignmouth, *A Letter to a Country Clergyman [John Owen, Curate of Fulham]*, London, 1805, p.50.
34. Diary, 15, 16 December 1791, 10, 12 January 1792, cited in R. I. and S. Wilberforce, *The Life of William Wilberforce*, 5 vols.,

London, 1838, vol. 1, 314–16, 322, 325–6, 334–6; vol. 2, 23.

35. This is based on printed subscription lists found in British Library Add. MSS 35129, ff.411–13; see also William Wilberforce Esquire Committee Account, Henry Thornton Esquire Treasurer, Hoares Bank Archive, London, *Customer Ledger 98* (1807–8), pp.353–6.

36. Hannah More to William Wilberforce, [15 June 1807], Oxford, Bodleian Library, Wilberforce MSS, c.3, f.89.

37. The evangelical vicar of St Mary's, Leicester, Robinson had co-ordinated a collection in the town on Wilberforce's behalf. Thomas Robinson to William Wilberforce, 11 September 1807, Durham, NC, Duke University, Wilberforce Papers.

38. Simon Houfe, *Old Bedfordshire: A Collection of 145 Old Photographs*, Luton, 1975, p.191.

BIBLIOGRAPHY

Adshead, David, 'John Soane's Designs for a Castello d'acqua at Wimpole, Cambs', *Apollo*, April 2003, pp.15–21.

Adshead, David, *Wimpole: Architectural Drawings and Topographical Views*, London, 2007.

Austen, Jane, *Mansfield Park*, 1814, ed. R. W. Chapman, 1923, 1982 edn.

Austen, Jane, *Northanger Abbey*, 1818, 1994 edn.

Bank of England Museum, text by John Keyworth, *Sir John Soane: Architect & Surveyor to the Bank of England*, Bank of England, 2004.

Batchelor, Thomas, *General View of the Agriculture of the County of Bedford*, London, 1808.

Bigmore, Peter, *The Bedfordshire and Huntingdonshire Landscape* in Hoskins, W.G., and Millward, Roy, eds., *The Making of the English Landscape*, 1979.

Binney, Marcus, 'Aynhoe Park, Northamptonshire: The Home of Mr James Perkins', *Country Life*, 16 July 2008, pp.81–4.

Bolitho, Hector and Derek Peel, *The Drummonds of Charing Cross*, London, 1967.

Bolton, Arthur T., *The Portrait of Sir John Soane*, London, 1927.

Bowen, H. V., *Business of Empire: The East India Company and Imperial Britain, 1756–1833*, Cambridge, 2000.

Brown, H.S., *Moggerhanger 1777–1977*, Bedford, 1977.

Brown, Ford K., *Fathers of the Victorians*, Cambridge, 1961.

Brown, Jane, The *Art and Architecture of English Gardens*, London, 1989.

Brown, Jane, *My Darling Heriott*, London, 2006.

Brown, Jane, *The Omnipotent Magician*, Lancelot 'Capability' Brown 1716–1783, London, 2011.

Byng, John, *The Torrington Diaries 1781–1794*, ed. C. Bruyn Andrews, 3 vols., 1938.

Carter, George, Patrick Goode and Kedrun Laurie, *Humphry Repton, Landscape Gardener 1752–1818*, Norwich, 1982.

Cambridgeshire Gardens Trust, *The Gardens of Cambridgeshire: A Gazetteer*, St Neots, 2000.

Collett-White, James, *Bedfordshire in the 1880s*, Bedford, 1986.

Colvin, Howard, *A Biographical Dictionary of British Architects 1600–1840*, 4th edn, New Haven, CT and London 2008.

Daniels, Stephen, *Humphry Repton: Landscape Gardening and the Geography of Georgian England*, New Haven, CT, 1999.

Darley, Gillian, *John Soane: An Accidental Romantic*, New Haven, CT and London, 1999.

Darley, Gillian, *Villages of Vision*, London, 1975.

Dean, Ptolemy, *Sir John Soane and the Country Estate*, Farnham 1999.

Dean, Ptolemy, *Soane Revisited (The Soane Gallery)*, 1996.

de la Ruffinière du Prey, Pierre, *Catalogue of Architectural Drawings in the Victoria and Albert Museum, Sir John Soane*, London 1985.

de la Ruffinière du Prey, Pierre, *John Soane: The Making of an Architect*, Chicago and London, 1982.

de la Ruffinière du Prey, Pierre, *John Soane, Philip Yorke, and Their Quest for Primitive Architecture*, National Trust Studies, 1979.

Drake, John, *Wood & Ingram: A Huntingdonshire Nursery 1742–1950*, Huntingdon, 2008.

Embree, Ainslie T., *Charles Grant and British Rule in India*, London, 1962.

Forster, E. M., *Marianne Thornton 1797–1887*, London, 1956.

J. W. Freshfield, *Remarks on the 'Counter-Address' to the Inhabitants of Hackney, on the Proposed Formation of an Auxiliary Bible Society; and on a Paper Entitled 'Both Sides of the Question' &c. &c.*, London, 1812.

Godber, Joyce, *History of Bedfordshire*, 1984.

Gore, Ann and George Carter, eds., *Humphry Repton's Memoirs*, Norwich, 2005.

Grover, John William, *Old Clapham: Based on a Lecture Delivered in the Year 1885 at the St Matthew's Church Institution and at the Clapham Hall*, London, 1887.

Guillery, Peter, 'Norwood Hall and Micklefield Hall: Works by Sir John Soane', *Architectural History*, 30, 1987, pp.181–9.

Hague, William, *William Pitt the Younger*, London, 2004.

Hare, Augustus J. C., *The Gurneys of Earlham*, 2 vols., London, 1895, vol. 2.

Heward, John, and Robert Taylor, *Country Houses of Northamptonshire*, (Royal Commission on Historical Monuments), London, 1996.

Hill, Clifford, *The Wilberforce Connection*, London and Grand Rapids, MI, 2004.

Houfe, Simon, *Bedfordshire*, London, 1995.

Houfe, Simon, *Old Bedfordshire: A Collection of 145 Old Photographs*, Luton, 1975.

Howsam, Leslie, *Cheap Bibles: Nineteenth-Century Publishing and the British and Foreign Bible Society*, Cambridge, 1991.

Howse, E. M., *Saints in Politics: The 'Clapham Sect' and the Growth of Freedom*, London, 1953.

Hutchings, Victoria, *Messrs Hoare Bankers: A History of the Hoare Banking Dynasty*, London, 2005.

Ingamells, John, *A Dictionary of British and Irish Travellers in Italy: 1701–1800*, New Haven, CT and London, 1997.

Inskip, Peter, 'Moggerhanger', *Georgian Group Journal*, Vol. xiv, 2004, pp.214–242.

Inskip, Peter, 'Soane and the Grenvilles', *Apollo*, April 2004, pp.17–24.

Jenkins, Roy, *Asquith*, London 1964.

John, Richard and David Watkin, *John Simpson: The Queen's Gallery, Buckingham Palace, and Other Works*, London, 2002.

Laird, Mark, *The Flowering of the English Landscape Garden: English Pleasure Grounds 1720–1800*, Philadelphia, 1999.

Ledoux, Claude-Nicolas, *L'architecture considérée sous le rapport de l'art, des moeurs, et de la législation*, 1804.

Leighton-Boyce, J. A. S. L., *Smiths the Bankers 1658–1958*, London, 1958.

Lever, Jill, *Catalogues of the Drawings of George Dance the Younger (1741–1825) and of George Dance the Elder (1695–1768)*, London, 2003.

Matthews, P. W., *History of Barclays Bank Limited*, ed. A. W. Tuke, 2 vols., London, 1926.

Mawer, A. and Stenton, F. M., *Place Names of Bedfordshire & Huntingdonshire*, Cambridge, 1926.

McCarthy, Michael, 'Thomas Pitt, Piranesi and John Soane: English Architects in Italy in the 1770s', *Apollo*, cxxxiv, December 1991, pp.380–6.

McCarthy, Michael 'Soane's "Saxon" Room at Stowe', *Journal of the Society of Architectural Historians*, xliv, no. 2, May 1985, pp.129–46.

More, Hannah, *Village Politics*, 1792.

Musson, Jeremy, *English Country House Interiors*, New York, 2011.

Musson, Jeremy, *In Pursuit of Antiquity* (Soane Gallery), London, 2007.

Musson, Jeremy, *Up and Down Stairs: the history of the country house servant*, London, 2009.

Palin, William, *Saving Wotton: The Remarkable Story of a Soane Country House*, Sir John Soane's Museum exhibition catalogue, London, 2004.

Parry, Eric, 'Wimpole Hall, Cambridgeshire', *Architects' Journal*, 26 March 1986, p.50.

Pevsner, Nikolaus and Bridget Cherry, *The Buildings of England: Hertfordshire*, Harmondsworth, 1977.

Pevsner, Nikolaus and Elizabeth Williamson, *The Buildings of England: Buckinghamshire*, New Haven, CT and London, 1994.

Phibbs, J., 'Landscape Survey for Moggerhanger Park', Report by Debois Survey Group, 2000.

Philip, Sir Robert, 'The Present Day Outlook on Tuberculosis', in *Collected Papers on TB*, 1937.

Pym, Francis, *Sentimental Journey: Tracing an Outline of Family History*, Sandy, Beds, 1998.

Rennie, Ian S. 'Evangelicalism and English Public Life, 1823–1850', unpublished Ph.D. thesis, University of Toronto, 1962.

Richardson, Margaret and MaryAnne Stevens, eds., *John Soane Architect, Master of Space and Light*, Royal Academy of Arts exhibition catalogue, London, 1999.

Robinson, John Martin, *The Regency Country House*, London, 2008.

Roberts, M. J. D., *Making English Morals: Voluntary Association and Moral Reform in England, 1787–1886*, Cambridge, 2004.

Rosman, Doreen M., *Evangelicals and Culture*, London,1984.

Shore, John, Lord Teignmouth, *A Letter to a Country Clergyman [John Owen, Curate of Fulham]*, London, 1805.

Smith, F. B., *The Retreat of Tuberculosis 1850–1950*, London, 1988.

Smith, S. R. B., Review of David Kynaston's *The City of London, vol. 1: A World of its Own 1815–1900*, 1994, *London Journal*, 20, no. 1, 1995, p.84.

Soane, John, *Plans, Elevations and Sections of Buildings*, London, 1788.

Soane, John, *Sketches in Architecture . . . Cottages, Villas and Other Useful Buildings etc.*, London, 1793.

Souden, David, *Wimpole Hall, Cambridgeshire*, London, 1991.

Stone, Thomas, *General View of the Agriculture of the County of Bedford*, London, 1794.

Stroud, Dorothy, *The Architecture of Sir John Soane*, London, 1961.

Stroud, Dorothy, *Henry Holland: His Life and Architecture*, London, 1966.

Stroud, Dorothy, *Sir John Soane, Architect*, London, 1984.

Stuart, James and Nicholas Revett, *The Antiquities of Athens*, 1762–1816.

Thorne, R.G., ed, *The History of Parliament: The House of Commons, 1790–1820*, 5 vols,London, 1986.

Thornton, Peter and Helen Dorey, *A Miscellany of Objects from Sir John Soane's Museum*, London, 1992.

Thornton, Thomas N., *The Thornton Families of England*, 2004.

Urwick, W., *Biographic Sketches of James Digges La Touche Esq.*, Dublin, 1868.

Waterfield, Giles, ed., *Soane and Death*, Dulwich Picture Gallery exhibition catalogue, London,1996.

Watkin, David,*The Architect King: George III and the Culture of the Enlightenment*. Royal Collection, London. 2004.

Watkin, David, *A History of Western Architecture*, New York, 2005.

Watkin, David, *Morality and Architecture Revisited*, Chicago 2001.

Watkin, David, *Sir John Soane: Enlightenment Thought and the Royal Academy Lectures*, Cambridge, 1996.

Whitbread, Sam, *'Plain Mr Whitbread': Seven Centuries of a Bedfordshire Family*, Dunstable, 2007.

Wilberforce, Robert I. and Samuel, *The Life of William Wilberforce*, 5 vols., 1839.

Wood, Robert, and James Dawkins, *The Ruins of Palmyra, otherwise Tedmor in the Desart*, London, 1753.

Woodward, Christopher, 'Moggerhanger, Bedfordshire', *Country Life*, November 23, 2006, 82–86.

List of Illustrations

DAVID WATKIN
PAGES 124–151

pp.124–125 Tyringham bridge, SM 13/5/4

fig. 1 SM P323

fig. 2 SM 28/1/7

fig. 3 3rd Earl of Hardwicke © National Trust Images/Roy Fox/17244

fig. 4 Thomas Pitt, Lord Camelford, medallion, English (Etruria), ca. 1780, by Wedgwood and Bentley, 1760–80.
©The Metropolitan Museum of Art/Art Resource/Scala, Florence

fig. 5 SM 13/7/1

fig. 6 Laugier 1755. SM

fig. 7 SM D2/9/3

fig. 8 SM P274

fig. 9 [The Yellow Drawing Room]: © National Trust Images/Andreas von Einsiedel/691873

fig. 10 [The Book Room]: © National Trust Images/Andreas von Einsiedel/691856

fig. 11 [The Plunge Pool]: © National Trust Images/Andreas von Einsiedel/2096

fig. 12 SM 8/4/10

fig. 13 SM Vol. 60/143

fig. 14 SM 13/5/4

fig. 15 SM 13/5/5

fig. 16 SM Vol.69/66

fig. 17 The Dining Room at Anyhoe, 23 January 1835, Cartwright, Lili (1805–1902)/
Private Collection/The Bridgeman Art Library

fig. 18 SM Vol.59/121

fig. 19 © Country Life Picture Library/Paul Barker/874259

p.149 SM P87 (detail)

pp.150–151 SM P84

JOHN DRAKE
PAGES 152–179

pp.152–153 Photo Peter Inskip

fig. 1 Repton, *Memoir 1814–15*, British Library

fig. 2 Repton, *Fragments on the Theory etc.*, 1816

fig. 3 Crown Copyright/English Heritage

fig. 4 Private Collection

figs. 5, 6 & 7 Crown Copyright/English Heritage

figs. 8 & 9 Lois Hunt Red Book Collection, Heveningham Hall

fig. 10 BLARS SH/400

fig. 11 John Drake

GARETH ATKINS
PAGES 180–199

pp.180–181 Reproduced by kind permission of His Grace the Duke of Bedford and the Trustees of the Bedford Estates

fig. 1 Reproduced by permission of London Borough of Lambeth Archives Department, lambethlandmark.com

fig. 2 Photo Peter Packer

fig. 3 Sierra Leone Collection, Sleo.0001.0001.0006.0001, University of Illinois at Chicago Library, Special Collections

fig. 4 Private Collection

ACKNOWLEDGEMENTS

This book would have been impossible without the generous funding of The Paul Mellon Centre for Studies in British Art and the Marc Fitch Fund; further funds which made the project possible came from the Alan Baxter Foundation, the Nicholas and Judith Goodison Trust, Sir Michael Hopkins, RA, and Lady (Patti) Hopkins, Sir Richard MacCormac, RA, The Portrack Trust, Helen Dorey and many other kind donors.

The Bedfordshire & Luton Archives & Records Service (BLARS) and Sir John Soane's Museum are primary sources of information and guidance on Moggerhanger House and Park; and particular thanks are offered to James Collett-White, Nigel Lutt and the Staff at the BLARS search room, and to Tim Knox, Helen Dorey and Susan Palmer at Sir John Soane's Museum.

For additional information our thanks go to Jonathan Pym, David Clifton, Peter Inskip, Jean-Pierre Brun, John Phibbs, Angela Simco, Dr Joan Anderson, Jenny Cooper, Simon Cooper, Monica Hill and the Rev. Dr Clifford Hill, and to the other Trustees of the Moggerhanger House Preservation Trust, both past and present.

The idea of the book was John Drake's and he set it all in motion and secured the first funds; special thanks must go to all the authors, David Baker, Dr Gareth Atkins, Jane Brown, John Drake, Peter Inskip and Professor David Watkin. Christopher Woodward kindly supported the application to The Paul Mellon Centre for Studies in British Art as a referee.

For the illustrations the generosity of the Soane Museum has been essential to this project; we are very grateful to Ptolemy Dean for allowing us to include his watercolours. For additional illustrations our thanks go to His Grace the Duke of Bedford, the Earl and Countess of Erroll, Mrs Lois Hunt, Mrs Jane Bretherton (for the Dawkins family), Mrs Phyllis Fane, English Heritage, the National Trust and to Justin Hobson of the *Country Life* Picture Library, as well as to all the individual picture libraries and photographers credited. We are also very grateful for the new photography by Peter Packer, and for additional picture research by Caroline Hotblack.

In the production process we are most grateful to Carol Anderson and Susan Palmer for their patient copy editing and proof reading respectively, and to William Jack for his excellent index. Additional support has come from Timothy Vince, Tracy Purser and Jo Smith and all who work at Moggerhanger Park today both on the staff and as volunteers.

Last but by no means least, we are especially grateful for the highly professional way in which John Calver, Gill Robinson, and all the staff at Healeys of Ipswich have brought this book into designed and printed form – and thank Sarah Ricks in particular for her elegant and thoughtful design of the book.

INDEX